HELP YOUR
TWENTY-
SOMETHING
GET A LIFE ...
AND GET IT NOW

HELP YOUR
TWENTY-
SOMETHING

GET A LIFE ...
AND GET IT NOW

DR. ROSS CAMPBELL
WITH ROB SUGGS

THOMAS NELSON
Since 1798

thomasnelson.com

Published in Nashville, Tennessee, by Thomas Nelson, Inc.

Thomas Nelson, Inc. books may be purchased in bulk for educational, business, fund-raising, or sales promotional use. For information, please e-mail SpecialMarkets@ThomasNelson.com.

Scripture quotations are from the HOLY BIBLE, NEW INTERNATIONAL VERSION®. Copyright © 1973, 1978, 1984 by International Bible Society. Used by permission of Zondervan Bible Publishers. All rights reserved

Library of Congress Cataloging-in-Publication Data

Campbell, Ross.
 Help your twenty-something get a life -- and get it now / Ross Campbell with Rob Suggs.
    p. cm.
 Includes bibliographical references.
 ISBN 10: 0-8499-4543-7
 ISBN 13: 978-0-8499-4543-4
 1. Parent and adult child. 2. Parenting. I. Suggs, Rob. II. Title.
 HQ755.86.C352 2007
 306.874--dc22

                                                              2006038460

Printed in the United States of America
07 08 09 10 11 RRD 7 6 5 4 3 2 1

{contents}

All of us who have adult children want to see them succeed. The problem is our idea of success and our children's ideas may be very different. They may see our efforts to help them as intrusion into their lives. Thus, conflicts arise which often lead to harsh words and broken relationships. Through my years of counseling, I have encountered numerous parents who are estranged from their young adult children, hoping that someday they will be reconciled.

The powerful message of this book is that broken relationships need not occur if parents can learn how to effectively parent their adult children. We are parents forever. The question is, "Will we be effective or ineffective in our parenting?"

None of us is a perfect parent. Therefore, one of the steps in effective parenting is to admit our own past failures and request forgiveness from our adult children. Such honesty can clear away the rubble and allow the potential for building a more positive relationship in the future.

Successfully relating to your young adult child does not come without effort. It requires genuine empathetic listening with a view to understanding your child's perspective. It involves accepting and loving your child even when you disagree with their ideas. When the young adult feels loved and respected, they are far more open to parental influence.

We cannot control the behavior of our young adult children but we can positively influence them. They can profit greatly from our wisdom. The question is how do we communicate our wisdom in such a way that it will be received and appreciated rather than rejected? Dr. Campbell has worked as a psychiatrist for over thirty years and knows the skills of interpersonal relationships. To the parent who is seeking help, this book is a treasure chest full of wisdom. I highly recommend it to all parents of young adult children.

Gary D. Chapman, Ph.D.
Author of *The Five Love Languages*

one

A GENERATIONAL PROFILE

Since you've picked up this book, presumably you have a son or daughter in the twenty-something age-group. And presumably what you want most is to help your adult child get moving in a positive direction in life.

Be encouraged—there are plenty of good strategies for parents to take. The very first strategy is to seek a clear understanding of the situation at hand. Most modern parents understand they are facing an entirely new world with new conditions, because they themselves were part of a generation that changed the world (called the baby boomers, the name generally assigned to the group born between 1945 and 1964). These parents aren't demanding that their children do things exactly as their parents or grandparents did; they simply want their children to *do something*. It sometimes seems to Mom and Dad as if the lives of their children are stuck in neutral.

Why is this the case for so many young people of this age-group? And what can we do to help them?

To start with, we can learn as much as we can about the world of our adult children. What forces from within motivate them? What forces from without?

Many people call them "twenty-somethings." Author Elina Furman calls them the "Boomerang Nation," because we hurl them out into the world, and they come soaring back.[1] Abby Wilner, another author, calls them "quarterlifers."[2] They have also been called the "iGeneration" (for Internet and particularly for that age-group staple, the iPod); the "MTV Generation"; "Twixters" (a term to describe being stuck between adolescence and maturity); and "Generation Y" (which means nothing other than being the follow-up act to their older siblings in Generation X).

Perhaps a good start would be to drop all the cute labels and attempt to see our children in a way that is more meaningful and less superficial. This generation is more than the sum of its influences, whether the Internet or MTV. Generational groupings in themselves are more helpful as media shorthand than as true descriptions of living, thinking human beings. Sure, to some extent your child is a product of 9/11 and the Internet, but in a much more profound and significant way, your child is genetically, spiritually, and emotionally a product of the home you have worked to maintain. No contemporary condition could approach the influence you have had by simply raising your child for the first two decades of his life.

> No contemporary condition could approach the influence you have had by simply raising your child for the first two decades of his life.

That's helpful to remember next time you begin to wonder if your offspring is an alien life-form of some kind!

Having said that, we can make some general observations about that group of young adults who are now in their twenties. What follows are a few of the hallmarks that help to define (at least for some observers) a distinct generation.

FINANCIAL CHALLENGES

Perhaps the most significant issue facing twenty-somethings and their parents is today's economic climate. A number of factors have conspired to create an atmosphere unlike any previously faced by young adults.

Twenty-somethings of the 1930s faced our nation's greatest financial collapse—a time when jobs were hard enough to come by. What makes the contemporary situation unique is actually more about *expectations*. That is, the parents of today's young adults have experienced unprecedented prosperity. They enjoyed the postwar boom of the late twentieth century and flourished. Some have speculated that today we have the first generation to face less prosperity than the one preceding it.

Think of it this way. The baby boomers are defined, more than any other factor, by their sheer numbers. During those years between 1946 and 1964, there was an unprecedented spike in the birth rate. Together these children came of age and entered the job market—and cornered it. Baby boomers dominate the workforce today, though many of them are finally reaching retirement age. As a result, young adults of the last decade or so have struggled to find their place—*particularly* given the heightened expectations of their successful parents, who naturally want their children to find the same success they themselves have enjoyed.

The title of a book by Anya Kamenetz is revealing: *Generation Debt: Why Now Is a Terrible Time to Be Young.*[3]

Not only have the jobs been elusive, but the cost of living has spiraled. Consider the increase in housing costs over the last several years. The National Association of Realtors estimated that this rate rose by 500 percent between 1973 and 2004—to a median price of $156,200.[4] You might argue that your child isn't looking for a home but an apartment. Still, could this situation have an influence, for example, on your adult child's plans for marriage, knowing that the American dream of home ownership is possibly out of reach? It is arguably the step of marriage that most influences young adults to "settle down" and complete the maturity process. Let's not forget that apartment rentals have also skyrocketed.

Factor in the issue of debt. Everyone knows what has happened to the cost of a college education. More than ever, families have depended on loans, and young adults often spend decades paying them off. Add to that the common problem of credit card debt, which is more of a contagion in our country than most people realize. Add all these factors together, and we find a generation facing the prospect of "McJobs" (their term for a spot at a fast-food joint or a mall store) that pay little while offering few or no benefits, and no viable course for paying off college and credit card debt. Meanwhile, a home or even a simple apartment costs more than ever. Is it any wonder we've seen a phenomenon of twenty-somethings moving back home?

Perhaps we're not telling you anything new. You may not need to be told, because you've lived it. Just the same, misery loves company. Sometimes it's good to know that you're struggling not in isolation but as part of a wider movement.

THE RECREATION/INFORMATION GENERATION

Another often-documented trait of twenty-somethings is that they've grown up in a world increasingly absorbed by leisure, recreation, and pop culture. Their parents have been more likely to pursue vacations more luxurious and hobbies more immersive than past generations, simply because they've had the means. Baby boomers brought in the harvest of hard work—their parents' and their own—and lavished it on their children. All of us enjoy giving our families the good life, but the results can have unintended consequences.

Boomers of the 1960s and 1970s nurtured their music collections—generally an armful of vinyl long-playing records. Their children often exchanged songs *in the thousands* over the Internet through the Napster file-sharing program (until the original version became illegal). Our children have been able to view any movie they want to see at any time, through Blockbuster, then Netflix. While their parents chose from three television channels, twenty-somethings grew up with one hundred or more through cable television.

This generation has come of age accustomed to a world of lake and beach houses, Rocky Mountain ski trips, and designer clothing. And don't assume we're speaking of only those from wealthier backgrounds; to varying extents, the prosperity of recent years has touched most Americans.

The advent of the Internet has personalized information more than ever. Twenty-somethings take the nearly infinite reaches of the World Wide Web for granted; what would their grandparents have thought about all this? Young adults personalize their social and recreational experiences through countless Web sites, or they express themselves through their own corner of MySpace.com. It's no longer unusual for young adults to nurture romantic relationships with people they have never seen, who may live across the world, simply through the magic of chat rooms—and don't forget that Internet dating services, which boil all the romance down to science and statistics, are exploding in popularity.

Why is all this important? Technology has indelibly marked the new generation of young adults. No one before them has ever experienced anything remotely similar to this coming-of-age experience. Our adult children are more absorbed with play and much less in a hurry to grow up. They are more acclimated to "interactivity"—that is, to experiences customized to their personality. Therefore, they are much less in a hurry to accept just any job. Finally, they are arguably (though not provably) more passive in nature, after excessive amounts of time staring at desktop, laptop, and television screens, all of which serve ever-enticing doses of a pop culture that is louder, ruder, and more insistent than ever.

AN AGE OF FEAR

Two words: *AIDS* and *terrorism*. The former left an immeasurable impact on the late 1980s and 1990s, and the latter has inarguably dominated the millennial decade. We're talking about the majority of a twenty-something's life. Death can arrive in the sudden, unexpected crash of an airplane into a skyscraper—or it can happen "quietly" through a slowly incubating disease.

AIDS isn't the only kind of virus that has brought modern America new strains of terror. What would we have thought of the computer virus thirty years ago? It would have seemed like the stuff of science fiction. A faceless criminal in unknown parts (he might be in Guatemala for all we know) has the ability to reach across the globe and destroy or steal the matrix of information that is your personal computer. As a matter of fact, the relatively new term "identity theft" can be seen as an apt metaphor for the times in which we live, where a younger generation searches desperately to find and hang on to its identity. Certainly that's the theme of these early years of adulthood.

This generation has grown up in an age of divorce and insecure relationships. Perhaps you've struggled as a single parent, and you will agree that it's a difficult and challenging context for raising children—though many, of course, have done outstanding jobs. The last two demographic groups of young adults have been branded with the label "delayers" because they're in no hurry to make a marital commitment. They have seen, from too close a vantage point, the pain that can come from marriages that don't last. On the one hand, it can be viewed as a good thing that twenty-somethings want to look before they leap; on the other, we sadly see that a pattern of superficial, sexually promiscuous relationships has not provided a healthy alternative. Either way, fear of commitment is a powerful component of being a young adult today.

> Technology has indelibly marked the new generation of young adults

When it comes to voting, the issue of ecology resonates strongly with young adults. They want to know the truth about global warming because these are their years in the sun. Twenty-somethings worry about what will happen when there is no more oil for transportation or air for breathing.

Certainly every age carries its own variations on the theme of fear. Some parents can remember the air-raid shelters and "duck and cover" instructions of the mid–twentieth century. But this generation had its adolescence during the era of Y2K, which brought the end-times hysteria that comes with every turn of the century. When the fears don't come to fruition, as they didn't with Y2K, there is a sigh of relief—but we all become just a little more jaded and cynical. The twenty-somethings of today are more cynical than any group in memory. Their humor, such as that of *The Daily Show* or *South Park*, is brutally dark and sarcastic. And behind sarcasm always lurks a hidden layer of insecurity.

DIVERSITY AND THE NONLINEAR LIFE

One of the great buzzwords of our age is *diversity*. We all know that our media, our schools, our churches, and nearly every other source of authority has redirected its language and policies to acknowledge a culture that is no longer homogeneous (if it ever was) in terms of race, creed, and culture. Twenty-somethings embrace diversity more easily than their parents. They're more likely to have grown up in multiethnic classrooms, and they're comfortable with once-taboo ideas of mixed dating and marriage.

Diversity, however, is a wider concept than demographic considerations. This generation has been described as "hypertextual." That word refers to the now-familiar Internet path of the hyperlink. We don't move through the Web in a linear way as often as we "surf": that is, we click on hyperlinks that lead in multiple directions. This is why we call it a "web." The links lead all over the place, and we crawl along whatever strands "stick." Previous generations have thought of truth and life in a linear, logical way grounded in some central authority—whether that authority be spiritual, governmental, traditional, or something else. In the post-modern world, truth is not seen as being universal and monolithic; younger people are more likely to view it as something as elusive, diverse, and open-ended as one's path through hyperspace.

In terms of simple life issues, that means a twenty-something isn't going to take a certain logical path in life just because others have taken it in years past. "The Bible says so" is not an argument-settler for them, nor is there much value in the idea that "we've always done it this way." Young adults see the world as a brand-new place with infinite possibilities. They are interested in options, and they want to keep as many of them open as possible. A "career" as a backpacking guide may be the answer for today, and tomorrow the answer may be something else. Today it could be an exploration of Buddhist ideas of reality, and tomorrow it could be back to Christianity. When they come to it, they'll click on the link that appeals to them.

> A twenty-something isn't going to take a certain logical path in life just because others have taken it in years past. Young adults see the world as a brand-new place with infinite possibilities.

Let's say a bit more about the spiritual side of things. We've seen younger people drop out of church in generations past, only to return a few years later with their children. This generation has fallen away in a much more radical way. Twenty-somethings see the mainstream church as being about yesterday's (linear, inflexible) answers, delivered through yesterday's communication styles. There are exceptions, of course. Some congregations have built services and ministries tailor-made for twenty-somethings with great success.

For the most part, the picture of twenty-somethings and church is more bleak. Recent studies show that as teenagers, more than half had attended church weekly. From high school graduation to age twenty-five, we see a 42 percent drop in weekly church attendance and a 58 percent decline by the age of twenty-nine—when presumably more of them are no longer transient students or delayers but steadier contributors to the workforce. If we do the math, we find that eight million current twenty-somethings who were once active in church will no longer be so at age thirty.[5]

It's a nonlinear life, to be sure. At least it's not the line of progress for which many parents have hoped and prayed for their children. That's why this book has come into your hands. Now that we understand a little bit more about the generation that our adult children call their own, what can we do to help them? How can we lovingly guide them without alienating them? Can the nonlinear journey intersect with the path to spiritual, emotional, and mental maturity?

I believe it can. What follows is a travel itinerary for this book's discussion of the various components of parenting your twenty-something child.

NOTES OF INTEREST ALONG OUR JOURNEY

In this chapter, we've introduced—in an admittedly simplistic and incomplete way—the unique and enigmatic generation of our children who are now in their twenties. Hopefully we've painted a backdrop—a landscape canvas—of the overall world of the Boomerang Nation. And we've introduced a few themes that we will revisit in much greater detail as we come to later chapters.

In the next chapter, we will begin to take stock of your child as a new member of the adult population. Or is he?* The issue is maturity. We are discovering that this virtue doesn't just happen; it doesn't arrive on a schedule. For today's young adults, it is likely to come more slowly and painfully for a variety of reasons. In Chapter 2 we'll consider the signposts of emotional growth and help you consider your personal situation, taking inventory of your child just where he is—and considering how to help him take the next step in the right direction.

Chapter 3 is about getting back to basics. Having reflected carefully on where your twenty-something is on a scale of emotional maturity, we will review some of the foundation stones of parenting as applied to adult children. Does parenting end when your child reaches twenty? Of course not! You will discover that it really never ends—and that's not necessarily a bad thing. In this chapter we will answer key questions: How do I now love a child who has reached adulthood? Is discipline still part of the equation, and if so—how? The fundamentals apply as time goes by, but they must take new forms for a new and more sophisticated age-group.

In the fourth chapter, we will consider the issue that has received the most attention of all recently: homecoming. Author Thomas Wolfe may have said that "you can't go home again," but twenty-somethings don't subscribe to that philosophy. In great numbers they are indeed moving back home, for reasons we have already considered in this opening chapter. How can you make the most of a situation ripe for conflict? How permissive can or should you be? What limitations should be applied? This chapter, a survival manual, just may save your sanity—and a loving relationship with your child.

*A note about personal pronouns. Because I can't know whether your child is male or female, I've chosen to alternate the personal pronouns "he" and "she" with each chapter. This is a little less awkward than using forms such as "he/she."

Chapter 5 is all about *you*. It comes as a surprise to some parents that they must carefully consider themselves rather than just their children and the problems of their children. The parent of a young adult is an aging parent, a less-energetic parent. The problems are more complex, but the physical resources are more limited. You must pay a price in time, energy, and anxiety. Are you up to the challenge? Many parents fail because they don't count the cost in advance. This chapter is a very serious reminder that you *must* care for your own needs, or your best parenting efforts will not work. Also, we'll look at some practical considerations for how you can care for yourself while parenting your child.

Our sixth chapter considers "interior" issues—and we don't mean redecorating your basement. Twenty-somethings represent the most medicated generation in history. "Meds" for younger people were once a rarity; now it is common for even children to use daily prescription medication, mostly because of advances in our understanding of the human body and its psychology. We'll look closely at the most common behaviors that lie behind these medications: depression, anxiety, eating disorders, and other symptoms that have become all too prevalent. As a parent, you need the best possible working understanding of the mental and emotional challenges that your child must confront.

Chapter 7 gives special attention to the financial question, which is so closely tied into the issue of twenty-somethings' moving home. Even if your child doesn't live under your roof, he may come to you frequently for financial assistance. How much should you comply? What are the limits? Many of our children have grown up in an atmosphere of prosperity where money for luxuries seemed unlimited. Now, unemployed or with a low-paying job, they still want to partake in the "good life." Quite often twenty-somethings learn to manipulate their parents to get that handout, perhaps without realizing they are being manipulative. This chapter shows you the warning signs and helps you learn how to deal with the issue of money.

Chapter 8 takes on a key issue of the twenty-something years: that of the career path. Are twenty-somethings preoccupied with the job world? The answer might surprise you. In many cases, they haven't thought seriously about the implications of work. They may have failed to take the long view. This chapter shows how you can work with your twenty-something, helping him to think about his proper place in the world of work.

Our ninth chapter is about the world of relationships. This can be a prickly issue between parent and adult child because our culture has changed so radically in just a few years. The rules, as perceived by young adults, are entirely different from those of their parents and grandparents. Many families experience terrible and prolonged conflict over the issue of relationships. What if your child brings home a serious potential partner and you disapprove? What are the right and wrong ways to discuss the issue? Again, the wise parent helps a child learn to think rationally and maturely. We will also deal with the problem of lifestyle disagreements.

Chapter 10 moves to the issue of spiritual parenting. It's too easy to fight with your adult child over the pros and cons of church attendance. As we have seen, twenty-somethings have largely given traditional religion a thumbs-down. At the same time, many of them are seeking spiritual experiences in new and puzzling directions in home churches or worship facilities whose true nature may be a mystery. This chapter contains information on how to help your young adult child think maturely about spiritual issues.

In our final chapter, we'll deal with the greater legacy of parenting an adult child. What's in store for his thirties? How will your relationship and responsibilities evolve with the aging of your child? Sooner or later, believe it or not, he will "get a life." Will he still need you? We'll complete our journey with a look at parenting over the later seasons of life.

Well, that's quite a journey, isn't it? I hope you're not tired even before we begin. To parent adult children, and to be ready to do so, requires your best energy and best attitude. Hopefully this book will give you fresh resolve and joyful anticipation of the work of parenting, which is often frustrating but ultimately the most rewarding task there is.

The Bible contains an ancient benediction that Jewish parents have held close to their hearts for thousands of years. The writer of Deuteronomy exhorted parents to use every moment of the day to teach children, even if that means binding the wisdom of God on our hands and foreheads. He especially anticipated that period of life when our older children are leaving the homestead—or perhaps returning again, with new needs and new doubts. The writer reminds us of the ageless wisdom and laws of the Scriptures:

> Write them on the doorframes of your houses and on your gates,
> so that your days and the days of your children may be many in
> the land that the LORD swore to give your forefathers, as many as
> the days that the heavens are above the earth. (Deut. 11:20–21)

There is great reassurance in this passage. When our twenty-something children reappear in our doorframes and gates, we feel a bit nervous and uneasy; so do our children. These words, however, remind us that even as times change, eternal values do not; true wisdom does not; even the hearts of people do not. We face new times with old, trustworthy ammunition—the greatest wisdom available to any parent or child.

And then we have the promise that if we hold to that wisdom, our days when "the heavens are above the earth" will be long and rich. We are never alone as parents, even when we are single or lonely or isolated. As sure as the sky covers our world, God covers our cares and worries. He is the one perfect parent, and he cannot fail.

Emboldened by that reality, we take our first step into the brave new world of parenting adult children. Shall we take it together?

two

MATURE ADULTS ONLY

There is an amusing fable about Adam and Eve. Don't look for it in the Bible—it's strictly extracurricular, though it carries a point worth considering.

It seems that Adam and Eve were exploring their new world, naming the animals, and trying to get up to speed on the whole nature thing. They noticed quickly enough that living things came in two forms: new and not-so-new. They decided to call the new living things *children* and the others *adults*. The only problem was that one became the other slowly and gradually. Exactly when did the child become the grown-up?

As they walked along, Eve noticed a beautiful butterfly. Its wings were like the many colors of sunshine. Surely something so beautiful would reflect maturity and wisdom. So Eve spoke to the lovely creature. "Excuse me," she said. "Can you tell me when a child becomes an adult?"

"That's an easy one," said the butterfly. "It happens when you get your wings. Before that, you're crawling around on these tiny little feet and you're all green."

Eve said, "Hmm. Makes sense!" And she hurried back to tell Adam.

The next day the two of them were walking along when they came across a low tree branch with a nest resting upon it. A mother blackbird was feeding a caterpillar to some smaller birds.

"Look," said Adam. "A whole nest of adults."

All the birds stopped and stared at Adam. "What do you mean, 'adults'?" asked the mother bird.

"Well, you've got your wings. Butterfly said that's what makes an adult."

"Wings? All God's children have wings," said the mother bird. "Butterflies are dinner for us, as a matter of fact. Never listen to a bug. The fact is, you become an adult when you leave the nest."

"Okay. We'll keep that in mind," said Adam, and the couple walked on. He and Eve were discussing their mistake as they came to a river, where a school of salmon happened to be swimming by. It was delightful to watch, and Eve called out a greeting.

"Good morning, little fish children!" she said.

"Who are you calling *children*?" asked one of the salmon, clearly insulted.

"Well, you're all still together. No one has left the nest. Blackbird said . . ."

"Blackbird? She can't even swim! And it's not a nest, it's a *school*. We're all on our way upstream for some wild romance— ever heard of children that can do that?"

"I see what you mean," said Eve, more confused than ever. "We should have checked with the fish first." But soon the couple came across a bunch of bonobo apes, who seemed to be having the very kind of wild romance that the salmon were so eagerly anticipating.

"Let me guess," said Adam, who was learning not to jump to conclusions. "You seem to be adults, but . . . ?"

"We're not," said one of the apes. "Plenty of kids have wild romance. Adults are the ones who make babies."

Adam and Eve said, "No offense, but are you absolutely certain about this?"

"Can you come back later?" asked the ape. "This isn't a good time."

So Adam and Eve sat down beneath a great old oak tree to think it all over. "So which is it?" asked Adam. "Do children become adults when their bodies change? Is it when they leave home, when they become attracted to the opposite sex, or when they become parents? I don't get it."

"None of the above," said the tree.

"Who said that?" asked Adam and Eve.

"Look," said the tree, "from where I'm sitting—or standing, actually—none of those things sound too good. My body doesn't do a lot of changing. I'm not likely to leave home. The sight of another oak doesn't get my sap flowing, and I have bark inside, not babies. Want to know the real truth?"

"I guess you'll tell us anyway," said Eve.

"Count the rings."

"We're folks. We don't have rings."

"Count the years, then. Same difference."

It seemed like a pretty good idea at first—just like the other suggestions they had been given. Still, it all came down to figuring out how many years were equivalent to adulthood. So as time went on, the question of adulthood basically depended upon where you hung your hat. Point well taken, but, it could get very confusing.

For example, in Europe in the Middle Ages, people figured that when young men or ladies got past twelve or maybe thirteen, they were adults. In Guatemala, there were a few who put the age of adulthood at ten. In the United States, the age kept moving back and forth, based on whether one could drink, vote, serve in the military, drive an automobile, or some other milestone. Eventually, to clear up a little of the confusion, people invented a handy new invention called *adolescence*, which began at twelve and ended at twenty—and it was up to the individual to find a nice spot somewhere in there to become an adult. Everyone was on their own.

The only problem was, after a while they started moving that age around too. Today, there have been sightings of thirty-year-old teenagers!

THE ADULTHOOD ENIGMA

What if you were asked to give a definition of the term "adult"? What would you say? Dictionaries generally handle it something like this:

One that has arrived at full development or maturity, especially in size, strength, or intellectual capacity.

If you think about it, that's a problematic measurement, isn't it? Who among us has reached "full development or maturity"? Perhaps in the designations presented—size, strength, intellectual capacity—there are measurable points. But can we really leave *emotional* maturity out of the question? I believe that as you assess the current status of your adult child, in terms of adulthood, the issues that will matter most to you will relate to this more subjective brand of maturity.

In the past, we didn't worry too much about the fine distinctions of when adulthood began. Though definitions varied, we used a number of predictable stages to indicate its arrival. These included the completion of school (either high school or college), entry into the career world, establishment of a separate home, and, of course, marriage. With a few exceptions, parents of thirty years ago could expect several of these rites of passage to occur at about the same time. In the middle class, a young man may go to work or enter the military at eighteen. A young woman would hope to marry or possibly work. In the more privileged classes, collegiate studies might delay things a bit. But surely when a young adult emerged from the university at twenty-two, it was understood that childhood had come to an end.

As we discussed in the first chapter, any number of factors have blurred that line. Many of these, particularly economic issues, are practical and objective. But in numerous other ways, ways more difficult to quantify, we are often frustrated with the progress of our children toward adulthood.

Consider Natalie. She is twenty-three years old and a particularly sweet-natured and affectionate young woman. She has always had that kind of personality. Natalie communicates well with both her parents, and with her siblings, most of the time. She is also quite intelligent and conversant in a number of fields. For example, she has very carefully articulated political views that she loves to debate. Weeks can go by and Natalie seems to be a comfortably functioning member of the adult world.

But sometimes her parents seem to touch some hidden nerve

in a conversation—perhaps what is in the beginning some relatively small dispute. Suddenly Natalie's anger escalates. She loses her self-control, shouts, and makes very insulting remarks. With a slamming door, she leaves home. On one occasion she stayed with a friend for nearly a week before reappearing a little awkwardly but more calmly. Quickly she was behaving as if nothing had happened, though her parents were still hurting inside from the remarks she had made during the dispute.

Is Natalie an adult? Perhaps someone would break down the reasoning this way:

NATALIE IS AN ADULT	NATALIE IS NOT AN ADULT
She is twenty-three.	She lives at home.
She has a job.	Her job could never support her.
She votes.	She is unmarried, has no children.
She has adult interests.	She has childish emotions.
She can be very responsible.	She can be very irresponsible.

It's not an easy call, is it? If we want to attach the designation of adulthood to categories of emotional maturity, then how can those be measured? Exactly what level of wisdom must be reached? And don't we all know adults of forty, fifty, or sixty who still display very immature behavior?

THE MORAL DIMENSION

Let me suggest to you a particularly helpful lens through which we measure our children's progress along the road to adulthood. That gauge would concern the issues of morality and integrity. I believe all parents desperately want to come to the day when they can look at their sons and daughters and view them as young adults who live moral lives and are people of integrity.

There was a time, of course, when our culture provided us help along the way toward those goals. It was simply taken for granted that the books your child read, the lessons she received at school, and even the films and television shows she watched all supported a basic, traditional view of morality that involved moral absolutes. Not long ago I discovered an old videotape of television shows from a particular evening when we had to be away from home. These weren't special shows but simply situation comedies and the like that we planned to watch with our teenage children.

> I believe all parents desperately want to come to the day when they can look at their sons and daughters and view them as young adults who live moral lives and are people of integrity.

They weren't even particularly excellent shows, but when I viewed the tape I was shocked by how much had changed. The 1980s sitcoms, even with their freewheeling humor, had certain moral values at the basis of each episode. They demonstrated such lessons as the truth that lying and stealing brought their own inevitable punishment—simple lessons of virtue, to be sure. But the viewers wouldn't have even realized they were receiving a "lesson." It was simply that our normal entertainment, as late as the mid-eighties, still conformed to basic standards, and there was an assumption that a comedy or a dramatic show should embody those standards.

This was about the period of time when your twenty-something child was very young. During the ensuing years, our culture continued a dark transition that had already begun sometime around the 1960s. Anyone would agree that the current climate, as far as popular culture is concerned, is very different. Even a few years ago we couldn't have possibly imagined the language and situations that are normally depicted in television and movies, not to mention in music or on the Internet.

I stress here, as I stress in all my books, that our culture is no longer family-friendly, and we absolutely must take that into account when thinking about the mental, emotional, and spiritual development of our children. In the case of young adults, of course, it is too late to try making decisions about the movies or TV shows they watch. We still must discuss the issue, however, because this is the social framework in which your child has come of age and must now find her way as an adult.

Your child stands at a confusing place between the values of her parents and the values of her social environment—which she more than likely understands are two very different worlds. By this time in life, she has a thorough understanding of the ethical, spiritual, and practical philosophies that you hold. You've worked to instill them in her, and she probably holds more of them than she even realizes—such is the power of parenting. Over time, she will come to realize just how much of the worldviews of Mom and Dad she has absorbed.

> Even a few years ago we couldn't have possibly imagined the language and situations that are normally depicted in television and movies, not to mention in music or on the Internet.

For the time being, however, she sees herself as making her own way in this world. She believes herself to be a much more independent thinker than in fact she probably is. During this period she will be particularly sensitive to direct advice. She may need it more than ever, of course, but she may not realize it. Your adult child will insist on being "dealt with as an adult" rather than having her decisions and movements dictated by parents. In fairness, few of us actively seek advice anyway; this stage, however, is a particularly sensitive one, just as it has been sensitive throughout adolescence.

As we will discuss later in the book, there is a fine art to guiding your twenty-something child in a palatable way that will not be impatiently pushed aside. For now, simply keep in mind that your adult child is struggling to decide what kind of person to become in this world—and ultimately, given your most loving assistance, she will make that decision herself.

Your child brings from adolescence to the threshold of adulthood a strong dependence on her peer group as she contemplates the world at large. Again, this is the continuation of a trend that first emerged during the teenage years. She looks at her friends in new jobs, in graduate school, in newlywed situations, in transitions of various kinds, and these are the measuring sticks by which she judges her own course. At this point in time, she is reconciling what you have taught her with what her significant friends, and the many voices of the world, are trying to teach her as they compete for her ear.

> Your adult child is struggling to decide what kind of person to become in this world.

This is why good moral training, from the time she was very young, is extremely important. Imagine two children: one raised in a very "loose" household with few restrictions and little moral guidance; the other raised by parents who were extremely motivated to instill moral and spiritual values in their child. Both of these children are now twenty-five years old. They are observing a number of their friends remaining unmarried while living together with members of the opposite sex. How will each of the two be influenced? I think you will agree that the first, raised by parents whose credo was "Let the child find her own way," will be likely to fall in line with the same behavior. The second has a far better chance of making moral decisions that will make her parents proud.

> Good models of responsible adulthood are ever harder to find.

Even so, the decisions are going to be difficult for your child. The outside influences are pervasive; the temptations abound. Good models of responsible adulthood are ever harder to find.

Yes, your child needs you more than ever. Will you be able to find the way to provide loving parental guidance to (age-wise, at least) a fellow adult?

THE VALUE OF INTEGRITY

I believe a central goal for parenting is to produce children who become young adults of *integrity*. I define that word in this way.

People of integrity are those who:

- Tell the truth.
- Keep their promises.
- Take responsibility for their actions.

As we've discussed, the new world around us has seen a tremendous erosion when it comes to integrity. Your child has no expectation that the world will be an honest place. Most of us discovered some of the harsh realities of the real world later on in life. Your child has seen it with her own eyes since childhood. She doesn't expect politicians to be honest, for example. In her lifetime an American president has admitted to marital infidelity while in the White House, then lied about it under oath. She has grown up with television shows devoted to ruthless manipulation of other people to achieve personal ends. In *How to Really Parent Your Teenager,* we discussed the phenomenon of cheating in schools. It is so pervasive today that many teachers simply let it go on.

Your child has noticed that few people today take responsibility for their actions. In this litigious society, a customer may sue a restaurant for the coffee being too hot, after spilling it in her own lap. Those who are arrested for various crimes make excuses based on some past influence or a dubious medical condition. No one wants to be held accountable. Very seldom do we observe public figures stepping up to the microphone to say, "I am wrong, and I take full responsibility for my actions."

Think again about the three elements of integrity outlined above. In this chapter, as we work on strategies for evaluating where your adult child is in the spectrum of emotional maturity, I propose that this is a good place to start. Think about specific examples in which your twenty-something child has handled various situations. Has your child arrived at a position of strong integrity? Don't be too discouraged by your own answer—remember that we have a destination in mind, and in this age many older adults have yet to arrive there themselves.

On a scale of 1 to 10—10 being perfect integrity—grade your child on the following questions. Think very carefully, drawing from as many incidents as you can recall, before answering each one:

_____ How truthful is your child when you ask her an uncomfortable question?

_____ How consistent is she in keeping her promises and commitments?

_____ When she falls short, to what degree does she take responsibility for her actions?

I might suggest a further exercise. Take the test again, but this time ask the questions of yourself. You need not share the answers with anyone else; however, comparing the two estimations provides a good backdrop in considering your parenting responsibilities. What about the parent whose child is aware that he cheated on his income taxes or tends to fall short on keeping commitments? Is that parent disqualified from being a moral guide?

No, not at all—though the job will admittedly be more difficult. Sit down with your adult child and discuss your own limitations honestly. Here's an example: "Jessica, it's not news to you that I have many imperfections. We all do. One thing you may have noticed is that I've let my pride get in the way at times. I can think of that occasion where I lost my job and vented about it for months here at home. I realize now that I failed to take responsibility for the things I did that *caused* me to lose that job. I simply diverted the blame rather than holding myself accountable. I say this because my dearest hope is that you'll do a better job in that department."

> Sit down with your adult child and discuss your own limitations honestly.

I want to be sure this point is clearly made. I believe that kind of honesty goes a long way in parenting. You're showing humility and transparency, and your speaking respectfully, adult-to-adult, will also be appreciated. I realize that many parents carry guilt about the mistakes they've made somewhere in the past so that they feel handcuffed in certain areas of parenting. There are parents today who remember youthful intoxication or experimenting with marijuana, and they are terrified about discussing such subjects with their children. But abandoning

> Honesty goes a long way in parenting.

any particular moral ground is not the answer, moms and dads. You were never expected to be perfect; your parents weren't perfect either, right? They had their own shortcomings, if different ones. One of the great things about dealing with adult children is that there are more areas you can discuss with them; they can handle the information better at this age because, believe it or not, they have figured out that their parents are *not* flawless in every detail!

At the same time, as Christian parents, we want our children to understand the wonderful idea of grace. We believe that we need not be imprisoned in any way by our pasts. Our Bible teaches that in Christ, our sins are not only forgiven but fully forgotten. That goes not only for past failures but for future ones as well. The most beautiful lesson you can teach is the one that shows how you have stumbled and then gotten up again with the help of God—wiser, stronger, no longer liable to make the same mistake. And as we will see in the next chapter, you want your children to know that your love is equally gracious. You will love them no matter what. Will you agree with or endorse every action? No, but the love is non-negotiable.

Gently help your adult child understand that leaving adolescence is not the same as entering perfection. She will still make her share of bad decisions, feel her share of heartache. Your door is always open to her, whether she lives in your basement or half a world away. And you can underline that truth by letting her learn from your own mistakes. Acknowledge them, and you have a great chance of helping your children avoid them.

EMOTIONAL MATURITY

What we've begun is an assessment of whether or not your child is a "mature adult." In review, we've discussed how difficult a call this can be. We've established the importance of moral maturity, and now we need to turn to emotional maturity. Again, there are no easy signposts. In some ways and at some times, your child may seem to be a full-fledged adult. At other times, you may be appalled at the emotional immaturity that leaps out.

While we want to avoid overgeneralization, we can't overlook the conclusion that this generation has grown up with more opportunities to miss some of the influences

> As Christian parents, we want our children to understand the wonderful idea of grace.

that cause us to grow emotionally. Can you remember a time when yards were filled with children on afternoons and weekends? Neighborhood kids congregated for touch football, or they rode in bicycle caravans. Where are all the kids today? Indoors.

There are fewer siblings in the modern family as well. Today's children have grown up largely indoors and alone, often with a working mother. The outdoors is less explored, partially because we are less trusting of our neighbors. Think of the decline in Halloween trick-or-treating, for example. We lock our doors and keep our children in sight. Meanwhile, the incentives to remain in the playroom include such things as all-day kids' television programming, computer games, and, of course, the all-pervasive air-conditioning on which today's children are much more dependent.

Younger people today seem to come of age with earphones strapped on their heads. They linger in their own immersive worlds of music and games. Relationships can even be with unseen people in chat rooms as more marriages and relationships are coming about through the Internet.

> Today's children have grown up largely indoors and alone, often with a working mother.

Again, not to oversimplify—not all young people have been irrevocably molded by these influences— but is it any wonder that some young people seem to lag in emotional maturity? Is it any wonder that twenty-somethings are often described as "isolated" or "detached"?

Many of the aspects of parenting necessary for developing emotional maturity will be detailed in the next chapter. However, let's close this one by exploring a few hallmarks of this goal.

SIGNS OF EMOTIONAL MATURITY

As we discuss these traits, of course, you'll keep in mind your own child's characteristics and the following descriptors of a mature, competent adult:

A Loving Person. The emotionally mature young adult will express love maturely to parents, to friends, and to those who are significant to her. She will also understand her need for love and receive it in a healthy way. Therefore, she is likely to be comfortable in a variety of social situations. She listens well, makes positive comments in conversations, and tends to build friendships. At the same time, as you offer a loving hug or an encouraging word, she accepts it graciously. Conversely, the immature adult struggles to express love. She will accept it, but only in a selfish way.

A *Self-Controlled Person.* We've already noted some examples of young adults who seem to possess maturity until some unexpected emotional outbreak occurs. Self-control is a hallmark of maturity, and the lack of it is a dead giveaway of immaturity. Mature adults chart their courses and move ahead proactively, living rationally and intentionally. Immature adults struggle in particular with issues of self-control. Overeating, for example, is a classic response to negative emotional issues.

A *Reality-Based Person.* Immature people are "spin doctors" of their own lives. They often blame someone else rather than taking responsibility. They may linger in denial rather than facing the real issue. Procrastination is another negative symptom. Immature people may fail to move ahead because of unrealistic hopes or a simple inability to engage the real world as it is. Mature individuals, by contrast, look at the problem squarely and consider various alternatives for confronting that problem.

A *Manager of Anger.* We live in a world that is incredibly angry. Immature individuals have never learned how to positively handle their anger. The anger is usually either vented in a destructive way or it "goes underground" for a while, only to emerge as irrational, passive-aggressive anger. Many young adults are carrying untended anger with them on the job front, into marital relationships, and everywhere else they go. The mature individual uses anger positively and then leaves it behind. She holds no grudges and keeps her relationships fresh and positive.

> The emotionally mature young adult is likely to be comfortable in a variety of social situations.

A Long-Range Thinker. While immature individuals live impulsively for the demands of the moment, mature people learn the power of delayed gratification. We all struggle to teach our children this basic principle, yet many adults have not learned it. That's why so many adults are in serious debt today and unable to finance their children's education. Mature people have the ability to see the "big picture" and live accordingly. This will come in particularly handy when making career decisions—for example, "Is this particular job one that will provide me the best future options?"

A Responsible Person. Mature individuals take personal responsibility very seriously. They understand that their reputations are affected when they fail to follow through. They hate making excuses and instead will undergo considerable sacrifices to accomplish the goal that is expected of them. Quite often, emotionally mature people will volunteer to help friends and coworkers because they also hate to see others become irresponsible.

A Relational Person. Emotionally mature individuals understand that life just doesn't work until and unless it becomes a group activity. They can sense when to step forward and take leadership and when to sit back and encourage someone else to do so. On the job front, they are team players who are valued by supervisors. They listen well and feel no need to compete or jockey for position. Obviously, immature people struggle tremendously at the point of personal relationships. It's difficult to watch them fail in this crucial arena because they generally can't understand why their relationships are so painful.

> Mature people learn the power of delayed gratification.

A Person of Integrity. We've already given this one special discussion, but it needs to be included on the list as well.

A Person of Perseverance. Mature individuals don't give up easily. The way they have become mature is through hard work and the development of inner toughness. They know that quitting once will lead to quitting again and again, and they also have confidence that if they simply keep working, success will be inevitable. Emotionally immature people have not learned that lesson, because they have given in to the pain of failure and never summoned the strength to keep battling. Our child may want to quit Girl Scouts or Little League after the first bad experience; we want her to learn that good things come when we learn to take the blows and persevere.

> Emotionally mature individuals are team players who are valued by supervisors.

An Independent Person. We certainly expect a two-month-old to be totally dependent on her parents, but we're sad to see this same dependence in a twenty-year-old. The independent personality is self-driven. She tends to go out and find the resources she needs without surrendering or demanding help. With a strong self-concept, she has a can-do attitude and tends to work well on her own, though she is equally comfortable in a group.

THE FINAL ASSESSMENT

What went through your mind as you studied that checklist? I hope you're not too discouraged. Keep in mind that this "mature individual" of ours isn't seen in public too often! In one way or another, we all have our little areas that need improvement. And it's highly unlikely that any twenty-something will grade A+ on every category of emotional maturity.

On the other hand, I think you'll realize it's equally unlikely that we will find a young adult who grades highly on one or two of those categories yet low on the others. These traits tend to ascend in tandem. They are highly interrelated to one another. A person who builds integrity is going to be a person who becomes more personally responsible, and vice versa. There is a great deal of overlap in these categories, but they provide a good starting point for thinking about your own adult child and the place she occupies on the road to mental, emotional, and spiritual maturity.

So this is where we stand. We've taken a look at your child's generation as a large unit—a cultural phenomenon. And in this chapter we've begun to think specifically about your child. It's highly likely that at this point many parents will say, "Where did I go wrong?" They will wonder why they didn't get the job done by their child's twentieth birthday. Just keep in mind that we're talking about something very common to our world today. If twenty-somethings were ever particularly mature emotionally in past generations (and it's debatable), we can be certain that few of them are so now. Parenting begins at a very definable place (birth), but the end never really comes—not as long we occupy the same planet as our offspring. What mother or father would say, "My children are alive, but I'm no longer concerned with or involved in their lives"? Would we really want to stop being a parent? Would we want to be unneeded in any way?

You love your child—you always will. Parenting never ends, and that's bad news and good news too. For just as there will be further challenges and problems, there will be even greater joys. Parenting is your greatest contribution to the world. There is still so much room for you to have a wonderfully positive impact in the life of your child.

In the next chapter, we'll go back to the basics—and find out how those basics are adapted to the wild, new world of parenting an adult child.

three

BACK TO BASICS

Some of us can remember when a bulletin board was a rectangular panel of corkboard. It was usually mounted on a wall near the office watercooler or in the corridor to the church sanctuary. Few people stopped to read bulletin boards; they held only yellowing newspaper clippings, sign-up sheets for potluck dinners, and mimeographed safety regulations.

Bulletin boards are now an integral part of the Internet, and nearly everyone reads them. In cyberspace, boards are "mounted" concerning any and every subject. In truth, they're not boards and they carry few bulletins. What they do contain is lively conversation from every quarter. Computer bulletin boards bring together people with specific interests. The users may be fans of a particular college football team or network TV show. They could be sufferers of a rare medical ailment or followers of a news story.

Parents of adult children are getting into the act too. One can find a number of bulletin boards dedicated to discussing the open questions of how to handle being a mom or a dad to young adults. Someone posts a note to the board, and it is called a "thread" because other posters reply, connecting their own observations to the opening note. Recently we conducted a Web search for "adult parenting" discussion boards. We simply navigated to the first one listed and saved the discussion topics. Here are the titles of the active threads:

- Charge rent to roommate's boyfriend?
- What's a parent's obligation?
- She wants to go to AUSTRALIA!
- PLEASE HELP!!! Made a big mistake with my daughter. :(
- She's home from college.
- One angry boy.
- Today is the fourth anniversary of Charlie's accident.
- Phone rings at 3:30 a.m.!!
- She's away at college.
- I can't get my kids to grow up.
- My daughter blows hot and cold.
- Relationships adult children.
- Should I continue to be Mom to "son"?
- My son and daughter are at odds right now. :(

The discussion titled "My daughter blows hot and cold" had been viewed nearly seventeen hundred times, according to data posted on the page. "My son and daughter are at odds right now" enjoyed similar popularity. The parents who have gravitated toward this one obscure discussion board are desperately helping one another through the daily crises of a challenge they never anticipated. When we think of parenting, our thoughts run toward helping little ones move through childhood, then adolescence. Very few of us spend much time thinking of those years beyond, because we envision our children as fully mature adults, ready to enter the world. They will *have* to be, right? We parented them!

But as we've all discovered, it seldom works out so neatly, and particularly not in this day and age. Exasperated mothers and fathers have come to me in the same way they have approached one another on the Internet: battle-weary and frustrated. For twenty years, the balance of power in the parenting relationship tipped in their direction, so

> We envision our children as fully mature adults, ready to enter the world.

they felt in control and at least heading vaguely toward the finish line of parenting. At its best, the household operated on a policy of love and respect; but in case of conflict, the parents could count on having the final word.

Now, it seems that all the rules have changed. After a disruptive argument, an adult child has someplace to go, at least temporarily. He can "crash" on the sofa of his buddy's apartment without telling his folks where he will be. That's part of the strategy; he knows nothing will wear them down like the anxiety of not knowing where he is or what he is doing with his anger.

As a matter of fact, adult children have a far wider arsenal of strategies and weapons for conflict with their parents. They are more subtle in knowing how to manipulate Mom and Dad, even if they don't consciously realize that manipulation is what they're doing.

Maybe this is how you feel. You may be saying, "I'm back at square one as a parent. My strategy extended to my child's age of twenty or twenty-two, but I can see now that we're nowhere close to finished. Where to now?"

FOUR FUNDAMENTALS

My response? The fundamental things apply as time goes by. While your child offers different and perhaps more daunting challenges as a young adult, the true basics of parenting have not changed.

What we need is a refresher course in the foundation stones of parenting—with a bit of polishing to fit the specifics of relating to a twenty-something.

> Adult children are more subtle in knowing how to manipulate Mom and Dad.

I have taught these four sturdy pillars of parenting for many years now, and I believe they apply more than ever. While they function in more direct and obvious ways when your children are younger, they are still operant in the years following your child's adolescence. What are these four areas?

1. Love and nurturing
2. Training and discipline
3. Protection from harmful influences
4. Anger management

You might be thinking, "Been there, done that." You'd be surprised at the extent to which adult children are still in need of a parent's guidance in each of these categories. The issues simply take different forms and must be approached with different strategies.

Allow me to demonstrate. Let's take a look at "the story so far" in your life as a parent. How have these four basic issues defined your task?

First, you've hopefully discerned by now that your child's most basic craving has always been to feel your love in a way that provides emotional nourishment. As a little child, he needed you to demonstrate it consistently; one blanket verbal assurance of "I love you" would not last very long. He needed to sit in your lap, to be hugged occasionally, and to have enough of your focused attention to know that your love for him was unquestionable. Even as a teenager, when your relationship became more complicated and often frustrating, he still needed the basic assurance that his parents loved him unconditionally.

> Parents themselves lack a basic understanding of how to manage anger.

Second, in your child's early years, your parenting was defined to a great extent by the areas of training and discipline. In the first two years, of course, there was the struggle of toilet training. Areas of discipline became more subtle and sophisticated over the years, but you continued to demonstrate that life can be successful and manageable only when we live by certain rules. If he refused to clean his room as a ten-year-old, there were disciplinary measures. If he got into trouble as a teenager, measures also had to be taken for the purpose of helping him learn a difficult lesson.

Third, your young child always had the need for protection from harm. A parent's most basic task is to provide shelter and security. This rule extended not just to areas of physical safety but to spiritual and emotional wellness. As a little one, you certainly didn't allow him to see certain television shows or movies. In his teenage years, there was the issue of poor influences at school, with the possibilities of substance abuse and sexual immorality. It was your increasingly difficult challenge as a parent to safely guide your child through a minefield of dangers in the immoral world in which we live. Your spiritual faith presumably had a great impact on your philosophy of evaluating harmful influences.

Finally, you discovered that your child had at least one special need: a strategy for handling the anger that everyone must cope with. In recent years I have written more about this issue of parenting (and of society) than any other. In an explosively angry world, fewer children are being taught to effectively manage their emotions. The parents themselves, I have discovered, lack a basic understanding of how to manage anger. We'll have a lot to say about the continuing task of teaching your adult child to accommodate and defuse his anger in a positive manner. I believe this one area can become the making or unmaking of a young adult in a high-tension world.

Those four areas, then, represent the central focus of all the parenting you've done up to now. As your children reach their twenties, obviously you have a different goal for them: to make a successful transition into adulthood. Yet I submit to you the proposition that you are still parenting your child in each of these four areas. Let's explore how each one adapts to the needs of adult children.

LOVING YOUR ADULT CHILD

This first category is the foundation for all the others; it is the foundation of parenting and of your life, for that matter. Please understand that every one of us needs to be loved and to be loved unconditionally—that is, no strings attached. We needed to know that the love of our own parents was a given; something as certain as the sun rising in the east every morning. If you felt that your parents would love you only if you performed or fulfilled certain conditions, then it would be very difficult for your soul to be at peace and your life to be emotionally balanced and effective. Your children need to be loved in that same way. It is my belief that virtually all parents love their children, but they don't always express it in such a way that their children know it is unmovable and unconditional.

> Every one of us needs to be loved and to be loved unconditionally—that is, no strings attached.

Does a twenty-something still care about his parents' love? Too often we mistakenly assume that's a question we got out of the way a long time ago. When he became a teenager, the focus of his world began to move away from the family room and toward the world of his peers. He seemed at all times to be striving for the approval of his friends. Now, as a young adult, he is moving to some greater extent into his own chosen world, even if he still makes his home under your roof.

For the reason that his life no longer revolves around Mom and Dad, it's easy to assume that love is a set condition to be taken for granted. This is truly not the case. Just as husbands and wives need to constantly demonstrate their love for each other, it must also be established unquestionably between parents and grown children—in both directions. Yes, your son may seem preoccupied with a fledgling career or with his active social life, but the affection of his parents is still a very basic need within his life. And it is often an *unconscious* motivation, just as it has always been. The younger child doesn't stop in the middle of play and think, *I have a need for Mommy's love.* The adult child doesn't have that conscious thought either. But at all times, in all our significant relationships, we want the reality of love to be renewed and reapplied, like a salve that cools us and heals the wounds of the day. Just as we attend church for a fresh touch from God, we return to our parents or our family members occasionally just for that reminder that someone is still there for us—someone who still cares deeply about us.

You'll notice the need expressed at key times. Your child is leaving on a trip across the country, and he wants to hug both his parents good-bye. He knows he won't receive that expression of affection and caring for a certain period, so he makes a point of claiming it now.

Another occasion would be when he has received some good news or experienced some positive milestone. Perhaps he got that important job he wanted so badly. Why do we embrace our loved ones during those congratulatory moments? It's a significant time, a transition of some sort, and we need to establish once more that our love never changes, even though our circumstances do. We feel joy, and we want to share that joy through a hug, but we also want to feel *their* joy for us. It's another expression of that love.

> Just as we attend church for a fresh touch from God, we return to our parents or our family members occasionally just for that reminder that someone is still there for us—someone who still cares deeply about us.

Another instance would be the period following strong words or a disagreement of some kind. After the dust has cleared and the emotions have calmed down (several hours, days, or weeks later), your child needs a fresh expression of caring from his parents. We all have arguments among ourselves, and we know with our rational minds that our commitment to one another is stronger than any disagreement. Still, we need it expressed behaviorally. Seeing is believing. Even a twenty-something craves the emotional nurture of acceptance by his parents.

The word picture I have used for this concept is that of the "emotional tank." Think of a child as having a fuel tank, much like an automobile. The fuel is the love of his parents. Your car's tank needs to be refilled regularly, and so does that of a child. The little one will come to you regularly for some kind of acknowledgment of love through your behavior—a smile, a hug or a kiss, even just listening carefully to him as he tells you something. Small children often misbehave when they have trouble getting that tank filled. They will cause trouble if that's the only way to get your attention.

> Even a twenty-something craves the emotional nurture of acceptance by his parents.

Young adults have an emotional tank too. You have one yourself. It is filled in different ways, and it needn't be filled every few minutes as it might be for a little one. But never assume that the time has come to handle your children as if they were business acquaintances. Be loving and affectionate with them, not just in word but in action. Your child received love behaviorally when he was in his early years. Words meant very little to him, so you had to demonstrate your love by acting it out. As your child has become an adult and more verbal in his communications, it's still true that behavioral expressions of love are the most authentic.

Therefore, let's examine how the most important expressions of love change in an adult-to-adult parenting experience:

EYE CONTACT

It's simple, it's basic, and it has a profound impact on the way we relate to one another. If we could measure the percentage of our conversation that is accompanied by positive eye contact (and researchers have done so many times), we would find that when things are well between us, we look freely into one another's souls through the eyes. When there is something we are hiding, when we are uncomfortable with each other for some reason, or when our minds are somewhere else, we look away.

It's simple enough: make sure you look your adult child in the eye, and patiently wait for him to meet your gaze as you converse. You'll find that by doing this you will connect far more effectively and more lovingly; you'll become far more adept at understanding how he feels and where he is emotionally; and you'll feel a deeper connection within.

> Never assume that the time has come to handle your children as if they were business acquaintances.

But it may take more concentration than you expect. When your twenty-something comes into the room, you may be thinking, *I wish he wouldn't dress that way,* or *I wish he would act more like an adult—he's not a teenager anymore.* As these thoughts cascade through your mind, you will unconsciously attempt to hide your feelings. Therefore, your natural impulse will be to look somewhere else as you converse.

But that's where love comes in. You'll simply need to remind yourself that your affection as a parent is unconditional. There are issues between you that will need to be addressed in their appropriate times, and they will need to be addressed more directly; you may not be prepared for all that now. Therefore, remind yourself of your affection for your adult child. Show the love through your eyes, and work at keeping positive eye contact as a good maintenance tip for your overall relationship.

PHYSICAL CONTACT

Too often we drift away from the habit of touching and embracing our children. It happens in most cases when the child reaches adolescence. Particularly in the case of sons to fathers, we feel awkward when our child seems to be growing up and becoming more sophisticated. As a teenager, he brings his friends to the house, and we know he would be embarrassed if we made a display of affection. As a young adult, he always seems to be in a hurry; always seems to have his cell phone held up to his ear. We feel the impulse to reach out and touch, but we're just not certain whether the contact would be welcomed or pushed away.

> All human beings need the affirmation and comfort that come through physical touch.

All human beings need the affirmation and comfort that come through physical touch. And we certainly need it from our parents, even as we (and they) grow older. Don't assume your child doesn't want a hello or good-bye hug or the kiss on the cheek that has always been a part of your greeting or good-bye. As a matter of fact, the aloofness of the teenage years should be fading away by now. Make an extra effort to offer appropriate physical contact at the right times, and you'll be taking one more step to help your relationship through this difficult period. After an argument or a conflict of some kind, be sure you use the comfort and powerful connection of physical touch in your process of forgiveness and reconciliation.

FOCUSED ATTENTION

Love is also expressed through our gift of time. We realize this more readily with our younger children: the father who knows he should go out in the front yard with his son to toss the football; the mother who knows she should take her daughter to the grocery store, even though it's more efficient to shop alone. Our children know we love them when we offer our time and personal availability to them.

What about twenty-somethings? It could be that now the tables have turned. Some parents would rather see their children move out and get on with their own families and their own careers. We were hoping to be giving our time to grandchildren by now.

But physical presence isn't everything. Time spent together isn't always time well spent. Even with a twenty-something living at home, we often sense that the relationship is filled with tension.

> Love is also expressed through our gift of time.

He comes in and watches a television show with us, but there's little conversation. He's at the family table, but we're really not connecting. What is happening is that we're together without being "on the same page." We're coexisting without cooperating. And let me add that now this issue has become a two-way street. Your adult child has to give you focused time, just as you give it to him. As with any relationship, this takes intentional effort.

So how do you give and receive focused attention? You simply make sure there are set times when you have no other distractions; you are there for each other. Maybe you need to go to a restaurant together. Maybe you need to say, "I'm not really enjoying this television show. Are you? Let's turn off the TV and just catch up."

A FEW WORDS ABOUT WORDS

Now we come to the crucial area of verbal communication. We have shown that children receive love behaviorally. Adults are obviously more verbally nuanced in their communication. When your three-year-old son wants to express or receive your love, he may run over to your chair and plant a huge hug and a kiss. Your twenty-something child has become more sophisticated in how he expresses himself. While all the behavioral issues (eye contact, touch, focused attention) are still quite important, the area of speech has now taken center stage in the daily communication that flows between you. So let's say a few words about how to talk to your twenty-something child.

First, realize the power of the spoken word. We communicate in many ways through talking, and not just in the substance of our words. There are facial expression, body language, and tone of voice to consider. Many parents find themselves too often driven toward argumentation with their adult children, just as often happened in the teenage years. Why does this happen? We tend to let the little tensions of our relationship creep into the conversation. We feel we are "conversing" with our twenty-somethings while they perceive they are being nagged or that there is some other agenda.

One issue is a fairly universal one: adult children want to be treated as adults. They would like to reinvent their relationship with Mom and Dad, who will now be considered something closer to friends and occasional advisers. In other words, they want to strip the authoritarian hierarchy out of the relationship because they feel that they've "arrived" as full-fledged adults, and they no longer need the day-by-day, decision-by-decision guidance of their parents. Besides, they believe themselves to be more up to date with such issues as technology and contemporary culture. They feel street-smart in this world, and their judgment is that Mom and Dad are a little out of date. The adult child says, "Respect me as an adult."

But the parents say, "Respect us as your parents." The biblical commandment to "honor your father and your mother" (Exod. 20:12) was in fact given to adults, who are commanded by God to respect their aging parents. Mom and Dad realize that their child is no longer a "child," but they feel entitled to the honor they've earned through years of tough parenting. They grit their teeth a little bit when they offer a word of advice and see it shrugged off or patronized with a reply of, "Sure, Dad, whatever."

> Adult children want to be treated as adults.

If the twenty-something is living at home, this adds a layer of complexity to the respect issue. The adult child says, "Respect my privacy and my boundaries." Mom and Dad say, "Respect our home and our rules."

Can you therefore see how some of these tensions slip into everyday conversation? We let the unresolved issues prey upon our minds, and by slow degrees, frustration builds up on each side. We are surprised to discover that some insignificant issue can lead to an argument. Words, even trivial ones, have great power because all of our emotions are behind them.

Monitor your tone of voice. Make sure it's positive and, yes, respectful, even as you ought to be respected. Speak gently, in a tone that moves slightly higher in pitch toward the end of a sentence (when the tone moves downward, it is interpreted as hostile or forceful). Be careful, however, not to talk to your adult child as if he is still a teenager or younger. Being spoken to as a child touches a nerve for nearly any young adult. Let your words show that you have a high regard for your child's opinions and decisions. Ask good questions. Listen well.

Remember that you are still a model for your child's personal development. He is watching the way you handle anger, the way you take an interest in others, and all the leading indicators of your own emotional maturity.

What if you do all these things but your child doesn't? That can be expected, of course, because he is the one who is in a difficult stage of transition. He is working things out and has unresolved issues, he feels uncertainty about the future, and probably has a certain amount of anger and impatience. There's no easy formula for handling a difficult personality in your house. Simply pray each day for patience and the self-discipline to avoid being dragged into an argument. At the same time, you will need to set rules for what kind of behavior will and will not be accepted. If your adult child seems bent on arguing and disrupting the environment, then obviously it's not a good idea for him to either live with you or spend extended periods of time with you at present—unless he can agree to abide by house rules.

> The adult child says, "Respect my privacy and my boundaries." Mom and Dad say, "Respect our home and our rules."

GIVING ADVICE

Related to the issue of mutual respect is the problem of giving advice. It's a built-in function of every parent. Since your child was tiny, you've been his guide, showing him how to walk, how to get homework done, how to go on a date, and whatever new rite of passage came up. Particularly in the teenage years, you began to see that advice was often deflected with a roll of the eyes, a mumbled response, an impatient "Whatever," or even hostility.

Even when you are old and gray, you'll still feel the impulse to be handing out constant advice. It just can't be helped—and, of course, there are times when your adult child needs it. But think about how you package that advice. Before you open your mouth to say, "Be sure you get a haircut before the job interview," or, "Don't stay out too late," ask yourself about the likelihood of the advice being taken seriously. Is it something your child has heard a thousand times, and will it serve more to irritate rather than to instruct? Does it suggest that you don't believe your adult child can run his own life?

> It's possible to drive your child away by "just trying to be helpful" too frequently.

There are many times, of course, when advice is important and very appropriate. Just be sure to find more effective ways to issue it. The more unpleasant the medicine, the brighter the package should be. Instead of "Be sure to get a haircut before the job interview," you could smile and say, "This is a really exciting opportunity. What kinds of steps will you take to present yourself?" In the context of his answer and the ensuing dialogue, he may think about the need for a haircut himself. Advice often takes the form of a command, but it is more effective in the form of a respectful question.

Some parents really struggle to ratchet down the advice machine; many of them don't even realize what a large percentage of their conversation advice is. We need to ask ourselves, "How much do I myself like receiving advice? Was I always receptive to it from my parents when I was a young adult?" Most of us aren't overly fond of being around people who are constantly telling us what we should do, and we avoid such people. In the same way, it's possible to drive your child away by "just trying to be helpful" too frequently.

A good rule of thumb is to pay attention to your own words. How many of them are polite questions that show interest and respect? How many of them are instructional and even patronizing?

To some extent, words make the world go around. They can set a positive or negative tone for your relationship. They can redeem a tense situation or they can inflict a long-lasting wound. Learn to use words as positive tools that promote love between parent and child.

TRAINING AND DISCIPLINE

As we come to the subject of training and discipline, I can already hear your question: "Discipline? For someone over twenty years old? How is that supposed to happen?"

For most of my career as a counselor and author, I've struggled to help people understand that much of the world uses the wrong definition of discipline. When I speak to parents of young children and speak this word, they believe we're talking about punishment. But discipline is not another word for punishment at all; it is another word for *training*.

> Discipline is not another word for punishment at all; it is another word for *training*.

Can you punish a twenty-five-year-old? It's much more difficult than when he was five or fifteen. Can you continue to train your child in his twenties? I believe so.

I've also labored to help parents understand that this goal of training is accomplished effectively only in an atmosphere of unconditional love. This is why we always discuss the home setting of love and nurture before getting to that question many parents are so eager to discuss—that of discipline. When a child of *any* age, including a young adult, does not feel loved, or feels *conditionally* loved ("I will accept you if you live the way I want you to live"), then it is very difficult to train a young person. However, in an atmosphere of love, grace, and forgiveness ("No matter what happens—even if I deeply disagree with some of your choices—I will still love you"), all of us listen better; all of us become open to change and growth.

How are you going to continue training a young adult who may believe he is already beyond the educational years of his life and needs no more training? It will happen in many ways, and we will discuss them throughout this book: helping him think through spiritual issues and helping him make lifestyle decisions, for example. Much more of this will happen through careful speech and focused listening and through the vessel of a mentoring friendship that exists between a parent and an adult child. But there are also times when your twenty-something will behave in ways that you as a parent must oppose.

> In an atmosphere of love, grace, and forgiveness, all of us listen better; all of us become open to change and growth.

Let's take a theoretical and common example while borrowing from a situation to which we'll devote an entire chapter later. It's the circumstance of allowing your child to live at home during his twenties. He tends to engage in social activities during the evening then sleep until ten or eleven o'clock in the morning. This tends to upset the housekeeping schedule that has been Mom's habit of a lifetime. By that time she has usually made up the beds, taken in the dirty laundry, and cleaned the breakfast dishes. Now her son is upsetting the familiar routine, and she is quickly becoming impatient. Even with an adult child, here is an area for training and discipline. How do you approach it?

REQUESTS

First, make sure your parent-child relationship has a solid and mutually understood basis of unconditional love. It's not something you can establish by quickly mentioning it in preparation for a confrontation; it has to be ongoing. Be certain you've been following the healthy practices mentioned in the earlier section on love. Then sit down with your son and discuss the issue in a positive and nonthreatening way, in which you carefully explain why his habits are causing a problem. At this stage you make a request that he make some significant changes in the time he goes to sleep and the time he rises. Keep eye contact, watch tone of voice, and listen patiently to his response. Mention that he's welcome to live at home during this period of time, but it's reasonable for everyone to agree on some ground rules.

Most of the time, when you are getting along with your adult child in a loving relationship, this will be enough to solve the problem. If he has even a minimum level of emotional maturity, he will have the basic consideration (and self-driven practicality) to clean up his act.

DIRECT INSTRUCTION

But what if he doesn't? A little time goes by, he makes a token effort, but within three weeks he has stayed out late and slept late once again. He strolls into the kitchen at 11:00 a.m. with a sheepish grin and says, "My bad!" attempting to make light of the problem.

To the parents, of course, it's not funny. This is the time to move to a slightly more forceful request—a *direct instruction*, or command. It's not a time to overreact and bring out all your emotional ammunition, because nothing good comes from that approach. However, you have a situation in which a reasonable request should have been respectfully obeyed. If there was one slip, you could have looked past it. But you can see that your son is falling back into the negative pattern you have brought to his attention. So you pick a good time for another conversation. You sit down and talk with him again, once again striving to keep your communication on grounds of unconditional love. Express your disappointment that the earlier request has not been honored, and let your son know that this is a more serious request that calls for his urgent attention.

> Make sure your parent-child relationship has a solid and mutually understood basis of unconditional love.

This time be more specific about your request. Leave fewer loopholes to be exploited. What time do you consider too late for him to be sleeping? What other conditions does he need to follow? Remind him that his parents are graciously trying to help him through this time and assist him toward a happy adulthood. Ask him if he has any questions, and be certain he has a clear understanding of what is now being insisted on.

SANCTIONS

If you move carefully through both these steps, and your requirements continue to be violated, there is obviously some kind of problem in the life of your adult child. At this point he's too old to spank, and he's very difficult to "ground." This is a challenge in parenting an adult child. You don't have some of the old resources that would apply to a younger child. What you do have in this case is a son living at home who is dependent to some extent on your cooking, cleaning, and shelter. You will need to let him know that if he can't follow the rules of the house, he won't be welcome here— and, of course, he will find there are rules to be followed wherever he goes. Again, your goal is not retribution or punishment, but positive training to help your young adult child become a mature adult of integrity and wisdom. If he can't live an orderly life under the roof of his own parents, he most likely won't be able to do so anywhere else. We will say a bit more later about how to handle these conflicts.

> If he can't live an orderly life under the roof of his own parents, he most likely won't be able to do so anywhere else.

PROTECTION FROM HARMFUL INFLUENCES

The most obvious work in the area of protecting your child from harmful influences is done earlier in parenthood. The younger your child, the more present and more protective you must be. A toddler must be in your sight at every waking hour, lest he put something dangerous in his mouth; a teen must learn to drive under your careful supervision, and you need to keep an eye on his music, movie, and Internet preferences and activity. The older your child grows, the more subtle and sophisticated your guidance must be.

But what about young adults? Can you really protect a twenty-something from harmful influences? Can you determine what

DVDs he rents, what Internet sites he views, or where he goes to meet friends at night? Certainly it's much more difficult, and some would argue that at some point—perhaps at eighteen or at twenty-one, depending on the individual—an adult becomes responsible for his own life.

I would argue that there is still some parenting yet to be done, even in this category. If you have a good, loving relationship, your child respects and appreciates your wisdom. You may not stand over him as he channel surfs with the remote, and you don't chaperone his dates anymore. In the past, you have hopefully given him more freedom and more autonomy as he earned it by showing appropriate responsibility.

But the time comes, quite frankly, when you can't control his every movement any longer, nor would you really want to. What you desire is for him to stand on his own two feet and make wise, moral decisions. You want him to live based on integrity and sound spiritual principles. And the best vessel you have for continuing to guide him in that direction is the power of persuasion through your personal influence.

> If you have a good, loving relationship, your child respects and appreciates your wisdom.

In recent books (for example, *How to Really Parent Your Teenager*, also available from this publisher), I have written very extensively about the moral decline of our culture. Parents today must really be vigilant in guarding against the corruptive force of a culture that is very negative and destructive. When your child was a teenager, you had to work much harder to see that immoral and dangerous influences didn't take their toll on the fragile young spirit in your home. It's a battle that by and large we are losing, and things have only grown worse for those who are now the parents of younger children.

In your situation, you watch as your twenty-something navigates the turbulent seas of that culture. Lower sexual morals are taken for granted. Issues of integrity are no longer considered very important. We rarely find worthy models among the political leaders, business tycoons, and Hollywood stars who set the tone for personal behavior. But you no longer have absolute power in deciding what influences your young adult child takes in. The issue is more complex than providing a family-friendly Internet filter or setting limits on R-rated movies.

So what can you do? Three things: listen carefully, ask questions, and discuss. Your child is unlikely to be completely comfortable with the condition of the world as he discovers it. He will bring his worries about it to you, and you'll have a chance to help him think through some of the issues with a mature mind.

I'll offer an example from my life. As a young man, my son David served as a business intern for a hospital chain. He was getting his first close-up look at the way things worked in the marketplace as he prepared for his own career. One day he was asked by his supervisor to consult with a competing hospital chain and use the opportunity to get into the competitor's offices and gather information.

> Listen carefully, ask questions, and discuss.

David was working on an MBA degree at the time, and already he was being asked to compromise his ethics. He told me all about it, and we were able to discuss the unfortunate state of integrity in the business world. David told me, "It's really sad to find out that this is the way people work, and that they don't even feel guilty about it. I guess this was my first test in business ethics, and I really hope I can keep from caving in when the next one comes." I'm happy to say that my son stood firm, as young as he was, and refused to carry out the request of his supervisor. He has done very well in business without compromising his integrity.

This is why you need to remain open and loving. When you let tension put a chill on your relationship with your adult child, you will find yourself locked out of the great issues that are going on in his world. Our children need our guidance, support, encouragement, and carefully given advice. It's so important to listen carefully to what is said and what isn't said.

> When you let tension put a chill on your relationship with your adult child, you will find yourself locked out of the great issues that are going on in his world.

Also, be on the watch for an opportunity to gently discuss (without our preaching) the issues of right and wrong, of wisdom and foolishness, of what helps to make us ultimately happy, and of what leads to misery.

Perhaps it bears repeating the three pillars of integrity we discussed earlier:

- Telling the truth

- Keeping one's promises

- Taking responsibility for one's behavior

Can you see how particularly relevant those attributes are in the lives of today's twenty-somethings?

- He is tempted to fabricate experience on his résumé. *Telling the truth.*

- He wants to get a divorce after only two years of marriage. *Keeping one's promises.*

• He can't get a job after dropping out of college, and blames everyone. *Taking responsibility for one's behavior.*

Many of the people and influences around him are in favor of lying where it is expedient to do so, of deserting one's spouse if it feels right, and of blaming everyone but ourselves when things go wrong. During this crucial time, he will make decisions that will help to mold the rest of his life. He will work from the foundation you have provided as a parent, but he will also hear many other voices competing for his spiritual and moral allegiance. To paraphrase the biblical book of Esther, maybe it was for such a time as this that you were given an opportunity to stand at the shoulder of your adult child and help to gently point the way down the correct path.

Do so by listening, by asking perceptive questions, and by showing wise alternatives in a nonauthoritarian way. You have a wonderful opportunity to help your child avoid the destructive influences of an ailing culture.

ANGER MANAGEMENT

Watch very carefully for symptoms of brewing anger in the life of your twenty-something. Once again, because of the massive moral confusion in our culture, there are relatively few people who truly understand the basics of managing anger. As a result, it's raging out of control in the lives of people all around us. Sad to say, parents have sometimes unknowingly made this situation much worse than it needed to be. Let me give you a theoretical example of the maturation of anger in the life of a young adult.

As a child, Bob was energetic, bright, and rambunctious—

sometimes a little difficult to control. His parents were rather "old school" in their beliefs that when we spare the rod, we spoil the child. So they were very severe in their punishment regimen. Bob knew that if he got out of line, the consequences would be very painful. In early years, that meant spankings. As he got a bit older, he would lose privileges (seeing his friends, for example) for lengthy amounts of time. The problem was that sometimes Bob wanted to defend his behavior, and he was never given any opportunity to present his side of the story. The punishment came, and no discussion was allowed. His parents had read books and attended seminars that told them they would be "conditioning" their son to be obedient and stick to correct behavior.

Bob felt a great deal of anger, and there was nothing he could do with it. The anger had no outlet because his parents would not even talk with him about these issues. Many times he felt unloved and desperate for affection. He got involved in church activities, which pleased his parents. He made high grades and thrived on the approval it brought him. But he believed he had to keep achieving or he would be rejected by his parents.

One day, when Bob was upset about things, he got into some trouble with a few friends who were stealing CDs from a music store. Bob's punishment, of course, was severe and extended. Eventually he put the incident behind him, and soon he was graduating from high school.

At college, he was off to a great start. He felt that because he was away from home, he could make his own decisions, and life was going to be incredible. But toward the end of his freshman year, he began getting into trouble again. He lost his temper and struck an instructor, and he also found himself expelled from his social fraternity. In everything he attempted, he would do well for a while before the cycle of self-defeat took hold. He transferred to two other schools, finally getting a degree at a small college near home.

As he started in the business world with a low-paying sales job, again he found himself excited, energized, and hopeful. The past was behind him; he had an opportunity to blaze his own trail now. And he did just great, getting two promotions rather quickly before, once again, the bottom fell out in Bob's world. He got into a bitter dispute with his supervisor, and ultimately the strained relations ended up in his being fired and having to look for an entirely different career—he had burned his bridges behind him in this one. To make matters worse, he had gotten married just when he thought life was going to be better for him. Now his marriage was on the rocks, because his wife had given up on trying to understand his unpredictable courses of action and emotion.

This is the composite story of any number of young people in our world today—people whose lives are dominated by the power of anger without even realizing it. Bob's parents, well-meaning and loving people, didn't realize that their "conditioning" approach to parenting, which was actually punishment-based, only created anger that Bob had no idea how to manage.

Anger must be dealt with appropriately; it does not dissolve or melt away. Instead, it brews deep inside us until it emerges in a new and irrational form that we call passive-aggressive anger. I have called it "stealth anger" because it is like a stealth missile that quietly but surely cruises through space toward its destination before exploding.

From his childhood years, Bob felt unloved and frustrated. (His parents did in fact love him, as parents nearly always do; but many parents don't realize how to make their children feel that love securely.) There was no outlet for his anger, so the anger simmered to a boil deep within him. Though he sought his parents' approval through church attendance, good grades, and other mediums, the anger came out in such incidents as shoplifting. At college and at the outset of an adult career, he always believed he could start with a fresh slate, but it wasn't possible, not as long as unresolved anger was dictating his actions. Until he understands the continuing causes of the disturbances in his life, he is doomed to repeat them.

Your situation, of course, will be different—hopefully far better. But unresolved anger from the past is something to watch out for very carefully. We believe that what is past is past; in actuality it has every possible bearing on the decisions and emotions we experience in the present. If Bob's parents had the wrong approach to handling anger, what is the right one? Is it to allow a child to run roughshod over the landscape and to vent all emotions fully? Not at all; that would be the opposite extreme. Venting of anger, by the way, is never healthy, never appropriate, and never resolves the issue. People buy into the myth that venting is a healthy way to "blow off steam," but in truth it only leads to the habit of more venting. It's not the right way to handle anger, and it doesn't work.

> Manage anger in two ways: *verbally* and *pleasantly*.

The right approach is to manage anger in two ways: *verbally* and *pleasantly*. These two goals are mastered in that order. As our children are growing up, we can teach them to talk about their feelings. But it won't be pleasant, at least not for a long time. None of us like to discuss unhappy topics. But it is better to talk about it now than to reap the whirlwind later in some irrational effect of anger, out of all proportion to whatever caused it. So we start out by learning to talk about our anger; then, if we really excel in our journey to emotional maturity, we learn to talk about it pleasantly—that is, in a tone and manner that are easier on those around us.

For all the reasons we discussed in the first chapter of this book, it's a tough world for twenty-somethings. Many of them live at home, and it's not their first choice. Many of them are struggling to get their adult lives launched, and that's certainly not their choice either. They must cope with a morally confused culture and a world driven by fear. For any number of reasons, your adult child could be angry and frustrated. Some of this anger may be directed at you, his parents. He could also have strong feelings generated by a romantic relationship that didn't work out or a career dream that is denied him.

Be loving and not intolerant as you begin to detect the presence of anger in your young adult child's life. Use open channels of communication to help him identify and examine the key issues in his world. This can happen casually; you don't have to say, "Sit down so we can discuss the greatest challenges of your life." That would be intimidating, of course. Instead, seek those casual moments when you're sitting together in the family room, or chatting on cell phones, or together for Sunday dinner. Listen carefully for the frustrations; they're bound to peek out and make themselves known, whatever you may be discussing. Though these resentments and pressure points may be unpleasant to hear about, *please* don't shut off those channels of dialogue. Your child is bringing you the significant issues of his evolving life. These are the matters that really make

> For any number of reasons, your adult child could be angry and frustrated.

a difference to him, and he is coming to you to be trained and counseled, though he doesn't realize it. Not only that, but you care enough about the implications of anger to help him now, even if it's not enjoyable to hear his words. You realize that if the anger within him goes unchecked and takes root, it will come out in some damaging form in the future.

At the same time, *watch your own anger*. Your child isn't the only one who is going through a trying time. You thought you were out of the parenting business, and now the end doesn't seem to be in sight. You're tired, and you have other interests you'd like to address right now. You feel an undeniable level of disappointment that your child is struggling to become an adult, rather than starting a lovely young family and bringing you grandchildren. Plus there's your own life, right? Everyone has problems, and are you supposed to put yours on hold while you deal with those of your child? When will it be your time?

These might be some of the thoughts that you harbor within. Anger builds up in parents too. You'll want to take care of your own emotions, perhaps even keep a journal of where you are with your feelings. Since all forms of misery love company, your angry adult child may try to draw you into his frustration. He may challenge your patience at times, attempting to provoke arguments. If you let yourself be drawn in, the battle is lost.

Take measures to avoid those confrontations. Walk away when you need to. Use positive self-talk: "I'm not going to let myself be drawn into this self-defeating cycle. I don't need it, and my child doesn't need it. I'm big enough to be strong and patient, to love unconditionally, and it's going to feel good when I resist the temptation to react!"

Anger builds up in parents too.

You'll be setting a good model for how your young adult child should be managing his own anger. Offer grace and forgiveness when your twenty-something hurts your feelings. And when you're the one who slips up—when you lose your cool or handle things wrongly—set the example of admitting your mistake and asking for forgiveness. What a powerful example you'll be setting for a child who is on the threshold of adulthood.

Yes, it's still possible to teach and to train, and in these very incidents, the ones we usually find unpleasant, we discover a silver lining: the opportunity to transform a tense moment into a teachable one.

I wish we had a lot more space to devote to this issue of anger. In all probability, it's a key issue not only for your child but for you—and for the remainder of your family and friends. An ancient Greek philosopher said, "Know thyself." In our time, we might say, "Know thy anger." Understand your unresolved emotions, and you have the key to your own emotional well-being.

> When you're the one who slips up—when you lose your cool or handle things wrongly—set the example of admitting your mistake and asking for forgiveness.

HAVE YOU GOT ALL THAT?

This chapter was a whirlwind course in the basics of parenting, adapted to the special needs of twenty-something children. Each of the major sections in this chapter had the luxury of its own chapter (or two or three) in past books, so we could give only our best attempt to summarize the most important truths this time around. I would recommend that you spend as much time as you need right here within these last few pages before moving on. So many of the issues we've yet to discuss can be handled effectively when we simply master the basics of these four categories. And without them, we're not going to do a good job. For example, if your child does not feel unconditionally loved, it will be nearly impossible for you to help him with career decisions, medical issues, lifestyle issues, or any of the other subsequent topics. Why should he take the counsel of someone who (he believes) doesn't unconditionally love him?

> Form the strongest bond with your child that you possibly can, and he'll be ready to listen, learn, and live in a way that will fill you with joy and pride.

The greatest truth in this chapter may be that parenting an adult child is not as separate an experience as you may have imagined. All the key elements—love, discipline, protection, anger—are still the main themes. But now you can't simply lean on holding the power balance in the household. "Because I said so" is no longer the magic phrase (and it was never very magical, if truth be told). There are very few courses of action you can demand that your child take once he becomes a mobile young adult.

So although you're still approaching the same basic issues, you will be approaching them differently. If you can't lean on forceful persuasion, you must lean on gentle persuasion. But isn't that the way it should be? Love has always been the most powerful force in the world. It can conquer nearly any foe, and it can turn back the tide of the most destructive influences in our society today. As your love for your child is sure, be certain he knows it, feels it, and thrives on it. Become more effective and persuasive in expressing it. Form the strongest bond with your child that you possibly can, and he'll be ready to listen, learn, and live in a way that will fill you with joy and pride.

four

WHEN JOHNNY COMES MARCHING HOME

We've already mentioned the famous quotation from the novelist Thomas Wolfe, who said, "You can't go home again."

Fewer people are familiar with the words of poet Robert Frost: "Home is the place where, when you have to go there, they have to take you in."

It is the poet who is being proven right. What parent is going to block the way when a son or daughter appears on the doorstep, in need of shelter?

When they come, we have to take them in. And they're coming in droves. Various surveys show that one half of all college students expect to go back home and live with their parents after they graduate from college. They know the state of the job market. They realize how expensive it is to rent, buy, or lease a roof over one's head. And frankly, they're used to the good life: a plasma-screen

TV, the swimming pool in the backyard, and a lifestyle that is more pampered than any generation in history has enjoyed.

The Boomerang Nation trend is not exclusive to the United States. It is happening in other industrialized countries, such as Japan, in exactly the same way. We've discussed some of the many reasons for this already, and there are many more. Some have to do with the condition of the economy, but there are deeper reasons as well—reasons that have to do with the way our culture is changing.

Various surveys show that one half of all college students expect to go back home and live with their parents after they graduate from college.

As civilization grows more refined and less driven by working the soil or struggling simply to survive, we become defined more and more by leisure. A few centuries ago there was basically no such thing as "adolescence." The term comes from a Latin root meaning "to grow up." People grew up quickly when the next meal could not be taken for granted; they had no time for what we now consider the normal adjustments of the teenage years.

As the twentieth century progressed, the age of marriage became later, and the social phenomenon of the teenager emerged—a group with its own subculture, its own measurable behavior, and a whole industry that revolves around learning to deal with it as parents. We've created new life-trends at the other end too: we have a large and active base of senior citizens, with such relatively new phenomena as care facilities and retirement homes.

The newest buzzword in the life cycle is "emerging adulthood," a label popularized by Dr. Jeffrey Arnett in an article in the journal *American Psychologist* in 2000. Dr. Arnett says that young adults "spend their late teens through their mid-twenties in self-focused exploration as they try out different possibilities in love and work. Essentially, a new developmental stage has been created between adolescence and young adulthood"[1]

Just what we needed: extended adolescence. The key term is "self-focused." Parents often become impatient with their home-bound children because those twenty-somethings seem to feel no sense of urgency about getting on with their lives. They are self-focused or (in the judgment of many parents) *self-absorbed.*

This new stage of life looks suspiciously like an encore of the teenage years, and sure enough, some have begun to call it "adul-tescence" or, in a term coined by James Côté, a sociologist at the University of Western Ontario, "youthhood." Dr. Côté writes, "It's the harbinger of a basic transformation of adulthood. The tradi-tional adulthood of duty and self-sacrifice is becoming more and more a thing of the past."[2]

Not surprisingly, Mom and Dad struggle to understand their child's mind-set about that traditional adulthood. They do under-stand the high cost of renting an apartment; they can see that even entry-level jobs are hard to come by. What they wonder about is why their adult child doesn't seem too worried about any of this; why she isn't in any hurry to get on with her own productive life, work, and family.

Again, there are many reasons, some of which are practical and some of which have to do with a culture obsessed with recreation, leisure, and plain old fun. At the same time, this is an educated and luxury-drenched generation. Mom and Dad may have emerged as young adults back in a time when they had a better chance for a good life than their own parents, who were products of the 1930s and the Great Depression. America was a boom economy for an extended period of time after the Second World War. Cities were exploding, freeways were extending their reach, and the business of America was more business. Younger adults in their early twenties were eager to get married, start a family, climb the corporate ladder, and claim their share of the American dream. The lure was the good life; why would anyone delay that?

The American dream isn't a phrase we use much anymore. The good life no longer seems to be in arm's reach. These are days of uncertainty, and the new generation has no confidence of doing even as well as Mom and Dad did, much less doing better. There was a brief period during the late 1990s when the dot-com revolution provided a thrilling ride for young adults. Entrepreneurs were pouring millions of dollars into such Web start-ups as Pets.com, which subsequently fell apart in the years 1999 and 2000.

It was a bitter pill for twenty-somethings who had counted on leveraging their superior understanding of technology in the new information age. They were going to be multimillionaires, but none of it worked out—and soon many of them were on their way home from Silicon Valley. They were home to live with Mom and Dad again.

DELAYING OR RETREATING?

As you formulate your strategy for making the best of a challenging situation, think first about the reason your adult child finds herself at home. There are many possible factors, of course, but these generally fall into two particular categories that should be approached in very different ways.

The first of these is a new kind of young adult we've already discussed—the "delayer" who is extending adolescence into early adulthood. This twenty-something has finished high school, college, or grad school and simply seems to be drifting rather than moving on into a healthy life. In this situation, the set of emotions and the level of maturity can be examined accordingly. Is your child simply immature and unprepared to take on the new challenges and burdens? Is she fearful? Is she confused about which direction she should go; or is she overly concerned with one issue such as a romantic relationship or the lack thereof?

The other major category is made up of not those who are delaying but those who are retreating. A great number of marriages are failing, as we all know, and a large quantity of them are failing in the early years. As a matter of fact, this is one reason the other group is more likely to delay such things as marriage. The number of divorces is daunting. Twenty-somethings are shying away from a 50 percent likelihood of marriage ending in divorce.

The "retreaters" may be coming home after a divorce or separation. They may be coming home after some kind of emotional trauma related to losing a job or having an independent business venture fail. Many of them, as we will discuss in

> The "delayer" is extending adolescence into early adulthood.

our later chapter on careers, are taking risks with start-up companies, musical or artistic ventures, or various enterprises that have a low likelihood of success. They have fewer job options to begin with, but there are many who are much more insistent on finding a job that reflects their personal interests rather than simply something that pays the bills.

The world is a hard place. New businesses fail quickly, and so do a lot of marriages. The only option left for a young adult may be the nest from which she originally took flight. This situation is starkly different from that of the delayer. One is hesitant to go into battle; the other is returning home wounded. If your young adult child is returning home after a crisis of some kind, then the key challenges for you will be those of emotional distress and healing. As most of us have noticed by now, the victims of broken marriages suffer deeply. It can be very difficult to console them and minister to them, especially when they develop brittle, bitter spirits.

In the case of divorce, there is also the problem that Mom and Dad suffer too. Parents of divorcees are unacknowledged victims. They mourn the loss of a son-in-law or a daughter-in-law, and they may also have a very deep-rooted anger at this young person who hurt their child. Mom and Dad feel the need to talk about it, just as the young adult does—but the last thing their child wants to hear is complaints about the departed spouse. Therefore, the parents don't know what they can or can't say around their child. They want to provide comfort, just as they did when their child was small and skinned her knee. Though she has come home for sanctuary, however, she seems to push her parents away. She seems to prefer grieving alone and nursing her anger.

> If your young adult child is returning home after a crisis of some kind, then the key challenges for you will be those of emotional distress and healing.

It's a very difficult situation for everyone involved. Parents are truly called upon to exert tremendous self-control, patience, and an emotional maturity of their own. There are times when they have to be gentle but firm, offering a message that says, "Your parents are here to help you. Our home and our arms are open to you. But please realize that the world goes on, regardless of your pain. It's a very difficult reality. We have needs and requirements, too, and while you're here with us, we need you to help us out in certain ways."

Those who come home after a crisis are the walking wounded. Life has dealt them an unexpected blow, and though living at home is a necessity and in many ways a comfort, it also is a constant reminder to their way of thinking that they have gone backward rather than forward in life. One day they were out in the world, building a life; the next they are back home in the old bed, surrounded by school pennants and teddy bears. They feel guilt. They wallow in low self-esteem and unresolved anger.

One healthy strategy is to find a way to exercise together with your twenty-something child. Walking is a wonderful idea. Exercise is therapeutic, and talking while walking just multiplies the benefits, if you manage the conversation in a healthy and positive way. As you walk around the high-school track or through the neighborhood, you'll find your adult child becoming more transparent, more willing to talk about her feelings. It will help you deal with your own too. During this and other times, be a world-class listener. Avoid interrupting to give advice or to make judgments. Ask questions, then quietly listen for long-form answers. Remember, anger is best managed verbally and pleasantly. I can't imagine a better forum for doing this than while getting fresh air and exercise.

> Exercise is therapeutic, and talking while walking just multiplies the benefits, if you manage the conversation in a healthy and positive way.

In the last chapter we talked about the emotional tank. Your adult child, the fresh victim of an emotional crisis, will need to feel love even more regularly and will need to feel it unconditionally. In other words, she is saying, "Mom, Dad, do you love a child who has failed? Do you love a child who caused you embarrassment around your church friends? Do you love me even if I have no idea what to do with my future?"

First of all, answer those questions for yourself. Surely each answer is *yes*. Express that love powerfully and regularly to your hurting child. Recall and reflect on the pain and failures from your own life, and draw on the wisdom you gained. Fill your adult child's emotional tank every day, reminding her that her problems have absolutely no effect on your love for her and that you would do anything to keep her from being hurt the way she has been.

> God designed her to lead a happy, mature, and successful life of her own.

Then, as time goes on, gently direct her to look to the future. She has come home to the nest like a baby bird with an injured wing. She is going to need to regain her confidence if she ever plans to take to the air again. You, too, will need to trust her. Just as you had to let her fly away once, now your goal is to send her off, happy and confident, on a new flight. While this may not be true of your case, some parents find that they enjoy being the mommy or the daddy again. They'd be happy if the adult child just stayed with them forever. This isn't what any young adult needs, nor what you need as a healthy adult. God designed her to lead a happy, mature, and successful life of her own. So don't get too comfortable! Love her, heal her, and prepare her for second flight.

THE "OTHER" CHILDREN

Sometimes twenty-somethings come home with children of their own. This provides an additional layer of challenge and complex-

ity to the situation at hand. More and more, we are seeing grandparents actively involved in raising a new generation of children.
Sometimes it is because one more marriage has broken up, as
we've discussed above. Other times, on an increasingly frequent
basis in today's culture, the children are born to single parents.
Your own children find themselves overwhelmed by either the
divorce, financial challenges, the difficulty of parenting, or some
other crisis, and they bring their children home to their own parents. What an adventure! Are you up to it?

I want to emphasize here that you must *not* miss the chapter
that follows this one, concerning taking care of your own needs—
physical, mental, and emotional. Those of us who are parents are
very sacrificial when it comes to our children. We would give our
lives for them, but if we try to pro-
vide more resources than we can
realistically provide, we will collapse, plain and simple. We're not
the people we were twenty years
ago. We tire more quickly, we have
physical and medical limitations,
and we still have our own lives, our
homes and responsibilities, and
perhaps our own spouses to care

> If you and your child take
> this challenge seriously,
> and work out detailed
> understandings of how
> the experience is going to
> proceed, there's no reason
> this can't actually be a
> positive time in your
> family life.

for. I have seen many well-meaning grandmothers and grandfa-
thers wear themselves out and end up with serious health concerns
because they tried to do too much. If you allow that to happen,
you certainly won't be any help to your child or to yourself.

We'll roll most of our discussion of home grandparenting into
the next chapter. For now, let's emphasize that if your young adult
son or daughter brings a child into your home, you need to take

serious stock of how the situation is going to be handled. You will need to find extra help outside your home, as well as being certain that your own child—the mother or father of your grandchild—doesn't abandon her responsibilities but does her share.

PRACTICAL AGREEMENTS

We've dealt with a number of difficult scenarios already in this book, but isn't there a possibility that you're going to do just fine when your child returns home? Of course there is. If you and your child take this challenge seriously, and work out detailed understandings of how the experience is going to proceed, there's no reason this can't actually be a positive time in your family life. We've discussed the underlying emotional elements of dealing with your twenty-something child: providing love and support and helping her understand and manage her anger, for example. But there are also very basic, very practical considerations involved in having a young adult live in your home.

These physical issues and the emotional issues, of course, impact one another. Little things, such as your child having a sloppy lifestyle, drive the emotional climate in the home. And the emotional considerations very much influence the practical elements of how we live. Even before your adult child moves in, you'll need to recognize the need to acknowledge and plan for these challenges. It's very unfortunate that in the heat of the moment, many families fail to take this crucial step.

Perhaps she comes home in the middle of the night after an argument with her boyfriend—or she comes home after college with the plan of moving on soon, but simply never moves on. In such circumstances, the problem is that suddenly there is another adult living in your home, affecting the household environment, and nobody has made the important arrangements and agreements so necessary to make this unexpected, unplanned development work. It's going to be culture shock on both sides, and tensions will arise quickly. Exactly how things are going to work, what parents and child can expect, how long it will last—all of these are undefined gray areas, and the result is likely to be chaos.

Therefore, it is imperative that you agree to hold a serious planning session before the fact, if possible. This is not a "come into the living room when you have a second" kind of meeting, but it's one in which you make an appointment to meet, and set apart plenty of time for discussion. Take notes as you plan together, and create an atmosphere of serious business. This way, both sides will take the challenge very seriously and realize from the beginning that, as with all important things, we will have to exert a concentrated effort if we expect the situation to work out the way we would like.

If your child is in the first throes of a crisis, you will want to delay the meeting until the dust is cleared and everyone can think clearly. For example, if her husband walked out on her yesterday, she will be in no condition to think and to make rational decisions about the future. You'll be focusing more on comfort, consolation, and whatever emergency steps must be taken. Just be certain that after a reasonable period of time has gone by (perhaps a week or two), you still set a time to hammer out this "homecoming manifesto."

Let me suggest how such a planning session might proceed.

BEGIN WITH LOVE AND AFFIRMATION

I would personally recommend opening with prayer, if you have a family that is comfortable doing so. Hold hands or touch your child's shoulder as you pray, establishing loving physical contact.

Thank the Lord for the positive opportunity that comes with this new and difficult challenge, and acknowledge that God uses all things for our good in the lives of those of us who love him (Rom. 8:28). Ask him to watch over your household in a special way during this time and help you minister to each other as you grow stronger and wiser through this new adventure. After prayer, take a few moments to verbally express your affection to your child. It's always a good idea to do this, and particularly in this situation when everyone is a little nervous or anxious. Smile, make eye contact, and say words to the effect of, "Living under the same roof, now that you're an adult, too, is going to be something we'll have to work at—on both sides. It won't always be easy. But right now, let's highlight the fact that we love each other. We'll find a way to make it work during the short season in your life that brings you back home to us. We're going to need a little give-and-take on both sides, and today we'll need to figure out some of the practical issues. But I know we can get along just great."

LISTEN

Don't forget that your young adult child has complex feelings about this development in her life too. As the parent, you'll need to resist the temptation to do all the talking. After you have opened the meeting with some words of affirmation and perhaps a short prayer, it's a good idea to ask an open-ended question to allow your child to express her own emotions and concerns. You might put it this way: "So . . . what do you think about all this? Are you relieved to be here, are you a little anxious? How do you feel about things today?" Just ask for general observations without getting into too many specifics at this point. There will be a time to explore those things in a careful and orderly way later.

THINK LONG-RANGE

Again, ask questions and listen attentively. Ask your child what she sees for her future. What are her career plans? What practical steps is she going to take to get those plans moving, and when will she take them? How can you, as a parent, help her with that? She needs to be considering the "big picture" rather than becoming engrossed in the here and now. Sometimes twenty-somethings find themselves drifting in life because they refuse to plan and to seek perspective. So it's a good idea to guide her thinking in this direction from the beginning.

ASK "HOW LONG WILL YOU STAY?"

Make it clear that you don't consider her visit to be a permanent one. It might be impossible for her to determine how much time she will need, but at least look for a ballpark figure. Will it be a month? Six months? A year? At this point she may say, "I have no idea! I don't know how soon I can work it all out." This is a good time to discuss the factors that have brought her to live at home and the factors that will allow her to leave. Is she employed? Is she going to find a job, or a better job? When will she able to afford her own apartment or home, and what kind of financial plan will allow her to make that happen? Even if life seems very uncertain at this point, it's a good idea to set an overall goal. You might say, "Let's circle the date on the calendar exactly six months from now, and make that date our goal for seeing you out on your own, starting your new life. I know you will be excited about making progress in that direction,

> As long as your child lives beneath your roof as a young adult, it's important to have a plan and a goal for helping her move out and move forward.

and the date will give you a concrete goal to work toward." Your limit could be three months or one year, whatever is appropriate for your situation. Also, the goal need not be an inflexible one; it could be adjusted forward or backward, as the situation and the new developments warrant. But as long as your child lives beneath your roof as a young adult, it's important to have a plan and a goal for helping her move out and move forward. Her eyes need to be on the horizon rather than on the prospect of giving up and staying with you.

WHAT ABOUT RENT?

This may be an appropriate question to discuss. When we offer them free room and board, free meals, washing and storage, and all the other things that go with being at home, then we may be making it difficult for them to leave; their situation at home is just too rosy. A rent payment might be a practical necessity for you anyway. Many aging parents, on fixed incomes, make tremendous (and unnecessary) sacrifices for their children who actually have a greater ability to go out and earn the needed income. Readers will have varying responses to the idea of charging rent to their children, but it can be an important element of the discipline and training that we discussed in the last chapter. Many twenty-somethings today need to learn the challenging realities of finance in the modern world, and they'll never do it as long as their expenses are paid and Dad's credit card is in their back pocket. Even a token amount might be a weekly reminder to your child that she is no longer "home" in the sense that she was as a teenager; now she is an adult and should be at some point in the process of building her own life. So consider a rent agreement. Have a definite date when it should be paid, such as the first of the month. Also, discuss what is being paid for—which brings us to the next point.

WHAT SERVICES ARE INCLUDED?

It's absolutely essential that you come to a careful agreement about responsibilities and provisions during this stay. Are all meals provided? If so, what time is your child expected to be at the table? Will she cook on certain nights? How will laundry be handled, and what are the guidelines for it? Will your twenty-something help with this chore, and should she sort her own things? What morning and evening hours are appropriate for her to come and go without disturbing the household? What use does she have of the house and its furnishings, for example, in entertaining her friends?

By now you've surely discussed in what part of the house she will live. It's ideal if there is a nice basement room or a garage apartment, because both parties will need a level of privacy. If she camps in a guest bedroom, however, you'll want to talk about issues such as whether and how loud the stereo can be played. Parents, be loving and accommodating yet very firm in these agreements. Your child is an adult now, at least in years. She may try to push certain limits, but remind her that this is a great trial for you as well as for her. This is your household, and you will need to be the decision maker; when she has a home of her own, she will be able to make the rules. The more rules and routines you discuss in advance, the better things will work.

> It's absolutely essential that you come to a careful agreement about responsibilities and provisions during this stay.

FINANCES

This is another subject that will have its own chapter (Chapter 7). Certainly it should be discussed in great detail, particularly if your young adult child is jobless and has very limited resources. Set your requirements (rent, groceries, etc.) accordingly. But if your child can't pay for much, that's still not a good reason for you to shower her with gifts or shop for her the way you did when she was younger. Again, you could be obstructing her maturation process. Who would want to leave a situation that was extremely comfortable? If she has a job, even waiting tables at a restaurant, then a certain amount of her income should certainly be going to help pay her expenses in your household. And if she can't pay for anything at all, then there are other ways she can contribute, such as cooking, cleaning, running errands, and performing various chores around the house. If this is the arrangement, once again you need to be specific about that. Let her know that every day she will be expected to do certain things on request, and agree from the beginning what some of those things will be.

PROGRESS REPORTS

As you end your first meeting, discuss a time to get together and review your progress. Two weeks or a month could be a good milestone. Go ahead and make an appointment, and plan to bring your notes from the first meeting. Go over all the items you've discussed, and look into how well these measures are working. Again, you'll want to meet from a context of prayer and loving affirmation. Keep things positive, but also encourage honesty on each side. If little annoyances are beginning to develop for you or for her, now is a great time to discuss them, rather than letting them increase to a crescendo. Subsequent meetings are also good opportunities to review your child's progress toward moving out and getting on with her own adult life. You can see how well she's progressing toward the long-range goal, and you can ask if there are any new ways you can help her move in that direction. I would recommend regular meetings—very frequently if the situation is tense and difficult; less frequently if things go well.

LAUNCH DATE

How long should you allow your twenty-something child to live at home? There's no simple answer to that question. It will vary from circumstance to circumstance. However, you and your child should always have an eye on the goal of her moving out at some point in the not-too-distant future. It's not because you don't enjoy having her around. It's not because you don't love her. It's because you do love her, and you know what's best for her. Bound up in

> Your twenty-something presumably knows that at some point she will have to pack her bags for good.

God's will for our establishing new families is the understanding that "a man will leave his father and mother" (Gen. 2:24).

This is for everyone's best: your child's and your own. While we as parents often miss our adult children and wish we would receive a visit or a phone call from them more often, we do expect an empty nest at some point, and we need the time and the space to rest and enjoy our advancing years. As for our children, they have a definite need to chart their own course. They cannot become healthy, functioning adults without going into the world to learn that role. Your twenty-something presumably understands this and knows that at some point she will have to pack her bags for good. You want to help her be concrete about setting a goal for when that will happen, even if it must be two or three years down the road.

But there are also situations where it simply doesn't work to have your adult children live at home, even for a relatively short period. Following are some of the reasons this might be the case:

- Your child has no sense of urgency or plan for the future.

- Your child is too disruptive a force in your household.

- You simply don't have room or appropriate accommodations.

- Your own health isn't up to the challenge.

What if you need your child to leave? You need to express that reality honestly and lovingly. Be careful to demonstrate the true reasons and the reality that you are not rejecting her. You still love her unconditionally, but you're simply unable to offer her a place to live at this point in time.

Some parents have offered to pay three, six, or twelve months of rent in an appropriate apartment, or to help their child search for affordable lodging somewhere else. In some cases the child has been able to move in with a sibling or another relative. Surely there's some creative option. The important thing is for you to realize that there are limits to how much hospitality you are able to offer. If housing your child is keeping her from becoming motivated to find a good job or complete her education, or if it is making you a nervous wreck for some reason, then you should not simply be a martyr and suffer

> Nobody likes the prospect of turning a beloved child away, but sometimes it's for her best and for ours.

silently. Meet with your child and explain what changes will need to be made and what the time limits are for making them.

I can tell you that I've seen this happen in many cases in which an adult child finally got her life on track simply because she was forced to do so. Nobody likes the prospect of turning a beloved child away, but sometimes it's for her best and for ours. Letting go is always an act of faith, for the parent as well as the child. Just remember that every day, some parent is making that same difficult decision you must make. It may be the most loving gift you could possibly give your twenty-something child.

A FRESH OPPORTUNITY

During these days when you do have an adult child under your roof, I encourage you to keep a positive frame of mind. Yes, it can be difficult in so many ways, as we have seen. The good news is that you are being given a final opportunity to put the finishing touches on your creation as a parent.

That task has extended longer than you thought it would, but consider what is possible for you as a parent. Your child is an adult now. You can talk to her as a fellow adult. You can be there beside her as she encounters those transitional issues we all must face as we enter the real world and become mature, independent servants of God and of one another. Why not make the best of this time to continue training and providing wisdom so that long after you are gone, your child bears the positive mark of your influence as a parent?

> As challenging as our world is, God is with us, and his wisdom is always there to help us prevail.

Deep inside, your child has many anxieties about this world she is entering. It can be very difficult to take those first steps without her parents there to hold her hand. She is worried about finding a life mate and about being successful in the business world. She wonders if she herself is cut out to be a parent. Therefore, she is looking more closely than ever at you, her own parent. She is more open to learning than she may seem; after all, she has come home. She has brought her life to you for training.

Take this time to pass on the wisest lessons of all. As challenging as our world is, God is with us, and his wisdom is always there to help us prevail. In the Bible, a wonderful example of parenting an adult child is the example of Paul and the young man named Timothy. The latter was raised and brought to faith by his mother and grandmother, but it was the elderly apostle who clearly served as a father figure. Paul wrote these words to Timothy:

> I thank God, whom I serve, as my forefathers did, with a clear conscience, as night and day I constantly remember you in my prayers. Recalling your tears, I long to see you, so that I may be filled with joy. I have been reminded of your sincere faith, which first lived in your grandmother Lois and in your mother Eunice and, I am persuaded, now lives in you also. For this reason I remind you to fan into flame the gift of God, which is in you through the laying on of my hands. For God did not give us a spirit of timidity, but a spirit of power, of love and of self-discipline. (2 Tim. 1:3–7)

Wouldn't you love to bequeath such a blessing to your adult child? Like Paul, you call upon the past (the influence of parents and grandparents). You mention your child's tears and your own joy in being with her. You encourage her to fan her own gifts into flame so that she can blaze her own beautiful trail through the world. Finally, you remind her that those of us who know the Lord have no reason to be timid about this world. God, the loving parent of us all, has given us all the power, love, and self-discipline we need.

I feel encouraged whenever I read those words, and I know I have the strength to prevail in the challenges of parenting my adult children. I hope you feel the same way.

five

CARING FOR YOU

Jim and Joan Benson are a happily married couple in their late fifties. For years, Jim has looked forward to retiring early. His cherished goal has been to leave his job on his fiftieth birthday and take advantage of his remaining years to enjoy travel, leisure, and all the things he's always wanted to do. Jim has saved his money, contributed to his retirement plan, and even built a small mountain cabin where he and his wife plan to spend plenty of cool summers.

Life has gone well for them up until now—not perfectly, of course, but they have no reason to complain. The last of their three children, a twenty-eight-year-old son, finally seemed to be settling down a couple of years ago. He had married, started a family, and decided to change careers, which required going back to school.

Then, eleven months ago, the Bensons' calm life suddenly became chaotic. Jason, the youngest son, called late one night to say that his wife had packed up and left. She'd gone back to work in recent months to help support the family while Jason was studying, and it seemed now that this had been a mistake. She had become bitter about the pressures of parenting while working. Suddenly she announced she was leaving, that she was not willing to discuss the topic further, and that she would be back for the children when she established a new home in the town where she had grown up.

Jason found himself in a jam. He couldn't make the mortgage payment without his wife's paycheck. He was too close to earning his degree to quit school. So he rented out his own house and moved home with his mom and dad. The two children, ages four and one, came with him, though their mother picked them up for a weekend occasionally. Jim and Joan, who have a modest home, scurried around to make accommodations for their three new residents. The two kids were placed in one extra bedroom and Jason in the other. That basically filled the house to capacity.

Immediately, Joan found that her life had totally changed. She'd forgotten just how much laundry two small children accumulate, particularly with the youngest in diapers. There were extra groceries to buy, but the greatest challenge was chasing two children around the house while her son Jason was in classes. Jim and Joan didn't have much time to commiserate. It was all they could do to manage the many new responsibilities that had sprung up.

Finances also caused anxiety. Understandably enough, Jason was shell-shocked. He still loved his wife, had been completely unaware of how unhappy she had been in the marriage, and would not give up hope of getting her to come back. He was depressed, unable to function even as a father, and desperately needed counseling. Not only that, but the oldest child was on two forms of expensive medication, and now there was no medical coverage because his mother had quit her job and left town.

All the extra expenses added up. Jim found that he had to borrow from his savings to pay for the prescriptions and the necessary counseling for his son. But that wasn't the last time he had to dig into his long-protected financial resources. Over the next few months, Jason's grades continued to drop as he had less time and desire to study. One day he finally gave up on his curriculum and the career direction he had intended. An old buddy from high school entered the picture at this point. The friend invited Jason to come in with him on a new business start-up: a trendy restaurant in midtown. As desperate as Jason was to reclaim a bright future and find a new hope, this idea energized him. He approached his father about a loan of considerable size. He was certain he could repay every penny in three years.

> Mind your health physically, emotionally, and spiritually. It's all you have, so you must care for yourself, or you'll be caring for no one else.

How could Jim refuse such a request when his son had been so depressed and had his heart set on this plan? The business venture seemed risky, but Jim knew he couldn't keep five people under his roof forever, particularly when two of them were small, loud, and needful of love and attention. He was worried about the way Joan was looking these days. She was moving rather slowly, hardly sleeping, and seemed to be struggling with depression herself. The children, missing their own mother, made constant demands on Grandma, and she ran up and down the hall, waiting on them like a slave.

Jim took out a great portion of his retirement funds, signed them over to his son, and resigned himself to the idea that he would be working several more years at the least. He also knew he might have to sell his mountain cabin.

Now the couple lie awake at night together. Joan worries about the children, who seem wild and unruly. Jim worries about whether Jason's new business is going to make it and whether he'll ever see his savings again. Both of them feel guilty for any negative thoughts about their situation—after all, this is their youngest child. What parent wouldn't drop everything and make any sacrifice necessary to help their child? That's the purpose for which they've always believed parents exist: to give their children (and now their grandchildren) what they need.

The reality of the situation for Jim and Joan, however, is dire. They are giving too little attention to taking care of themselves and each other. Their friends at church ask them about their health, but Jim and Joan just shrug with a hint of sadness in their eyes and say, "Us? We're fine! We don't have time to get sick or worry about ourselves."

What crisis will be required for this couple to realize the limitations of their personal resources? If one of them becomes disabled through fatigue or illness, what then? They certainly won't be able to help their son and grandchildren in that event. Jim and Joan Benson need to stop, look, and listen—that is, stop running, look in the mirror, and listen to what their bodies and emotions are saying. The message is, "Mind your health physically, emotionally, and spiritually. It's all you have, so you must care for yourself, or you'll be caring for no one else."

WHAT YOU OWE YOURSELF— AND YOUR CHILDREN

As I look at the world around me, and particularly my own circle of friends, there is one strong observation that brings me great sadness. It seems to me that people will not take care of themselves these days.

I'm not certain why this is so; perhaps we're just in too great a hurry. Perhaps the goals that life places before us seem too urgent. People I know are pushing so hard toward some desirable attainment or other that they forget the basic truth: we have this one body, this one soul, this one emotional matrix, and we can't upgrade; we can't make replacements. I can honestly say that I grieve for friends I have lost who would still be with us if they had simply attended to their own personal needs.

We advise others to do it, of course. We're always counseling our friends and loved ones that they should get a regular physical examination, that they should eat better, that they should get more sleep, and so on. We talk a good game until it comes to that very important acquaintance whose tired face we see in the mirror. We actually tell our own children to take better care of themselves even as we struggle with the same issues. It may be that many of us were raised by seemingly heroic parents who were almost martyrs, sacrificing themselves for us, and always focused on others instead of themselves. As a result, we now confuse self-care with selfishness. Nothing could be farther from the truth.

> We talk a good game until it comes to that very important acquaintance whose tired face we see in the mirror.

Therefore, readers, consider this my urgent plea to you. Take stock of your own needs right now, before the damage is done. Considering you have bought this book, you must have significant concerns about the challenge of relating to your twenty-something child and getting him moving in the right direction. That's one of the tallest orders I know, so think about it this way. For the sake of argument, let's say your health is optimal right now—nearly perfect. Let's say you are emotionally happy and vibrant, mentally and spiritually strong. Is it therefore going to be an easy matter to help your adult child?

No, it's not. It's *still* a considerable challenge no matter how excellent your own condition is.

Now consider *reality*. I would venture to guess that your physical health is not exactly perfect, not if you're like most of us today. If you have at least one adult child, then you are most likely at least forty years old. Already you've lost a good bit of the energy and strength you had when you were the age your child is now. You may have medical concerns, either mild or more serious. You also have your ups and downs emotionally, as all of us do. Studies indicate that 50 percent of us use at least one prescription medication, and one in six of us use at least three. Between 1988 and 2000, adult use of antidepressants tripled.[1] So unless you are quite a remarkable man or woman by today's standards, you aren't enjoying absolutely perfect physical, spiritual, and emotional health.

> You should have a healthy self-love, which is not selfish at all; God loves you, and therefore you should love yourself.

Reality suggests, then, that you had better care for your personal needs, and care for them as completely and as effectively as possible. You should have a healthy self-love, which is not selfish at all; God loves you, and therefore you should love yourself. Also, loving your family requires you to take care of yourself. It is not going to happen miraculously just because your child has a great need. The Lord will provide for you, but you must do your part. He gives each of us the opportunity to get the help we need, and he gives us enough good common sense to know how to get it.

You began reading this book because you wanted to care for someone else—your adult child. But in this chapter, I plan to show you how to care for yourself. That's a prerequisite to everything else. Please read each of these sections reflectively, then give special attention to the one titled "Are You Up to the Task?"

CARE FOR YOUR BODY

It all begins, of course, with that physical receptacle of everything that is you: your body. There is more involved in caring for ourselves physically than we like to imagine, but as we grow older, the requirements are even greater. Younger people can eat more recklessly without showing the ill effects, for example. They can handle fewer hours of sleep at certain stages—not that they should do any of these things, but we all get into bad habits early in life. The young are less likely to need medication, though more of them are, in fact, using it these days.

Some of us are actually in a state of denial that we are growing older. The first step in taking better care of ourselves is to acknowledge that fact: "I'm not as young as I used to be. Tomorrow I'll be just a little older still. Every year that passes, I need to take better care of this body if I want it to last." Unfortunately, we often learn the truth of that need only by making the mistake of not taking sufficient care of our bodies—and it's very difficult to undo the damage.

Have you thought about your diet lately? Few of us eat the way we should. Quite often, parents do a better job of eating square meals when there are growing children around the house. As the kids grow up and leave, we have fewer people to cook for. We're less motivated to take pains with a good meal, and we begin to eat more carelessly, picking up a hamburger or eating, say, canned soups that are filled with salt. We also tend to have a more sedentary lifestyle. The result, of course, is higher body fat, which has an impact on the health of the heart, blood pressure, and other key factors of health.

Our metabolism slows down after we reach the age of thirty, reducing the amount of calories required to sustain the body. But we tend not to reduce our caloric intake, and therefore the result over time is to become overweight and then obese. During the last twenty-five years, obesity prevalence has doubled in adults, and the prevalence of being overweight has tripled in children and adolescents.[2] The current baby boomer generation, as it reaches retirement age, will raise the obesity rate even further.

You need not follow a complicated diet, though a program such as Weight Watchers can be very healthy and encouraging. The best bet is to ask your doctor to recommend a good diet program, containing the right foods in the right quantities.

Exercise is the next component of physical health. Are you involved in regular, strenuous exercise of some kind right now, two to three times per week? The right diet combined with the right exercise program will have a profound effect on your wellness and your ability to help your adult child, as well as every other meaningful part of your life. Again, an expensive gymnasium membership is unnecessary. A helpful exercise regimen can be as simple as a good walk, if you move at an aggressive pace and walk at least a mile several times per week.

As we've discussed, there are emotional fringe benefits to physical exercise, and it can even be a pleasant time of companionship with a spouse, a neighbor, or your adult child. Sometimes it's amazing to discover how much we simply need to get outdoors and see the sunshine, which physically affects our mood. We need to feel the fresh air, stimulate the cardiovascular system, and see that there's a whole world out there beyond the challenges that overwhelm us indoors. If you're coping with a stressful life situation right now, or if there has been some kind of significant change in your life, be absolutely certain that you make time for some healthy exercise. It's essential.

The exercise will help you in another area: physical rest. Many people believe the myth that poor sleep simply comes with increasing age. Recent research suggests otherwise. Older adults may actually sleep *better* than younger people—*if* their overall quality of life is good. A National Sleep Foundation study found healthy older adults tend to get a good night's rest, while the greater the number of diagnosed medical conditions, the more likely they are to report sleep problems. At the same time, adults who see themselves as being positive and optimistic, and who are active and social, tend to sleep seven to nine hours and report no sleeping problems.[3]

> Aging doesn't cause poor sleep, but poor attention to health does.

Therefore, aging doesn't cause poor sleep, but poor attention to health does.

Are you getting the rest you need? Do you find that you lie awake worrying about the problems of the day? Sleep disorders are a difficult problem, and you may need to consult your doctor for assistance. However, it's also true that if you eat right, exercise, and effectively handle the emotions of your current life with a strong spiritual outlook, then you have already taken the right steps toward getting the rest you desperately need for your life, and particularly for your efforts in parenting.

Here are the basic steps to take if you're serious about getting better sleep. First, avoid any beverage with caffeine after noon. Second, establish a regular bedtime and a regular time to rise so that your body will know what to expect and take the right cues when it's time to sleep or rise. Avoid any kind of mental stimulation the hour before bedtime, such as certain television shows or dwelling on the issues of your current stress. Do all you can to relax during that last hour, particularly by reading or taking a warm bath. If you lie awake in the middle of the night, don't work too hard to get to sleep; simply turn on the light and read until you feel drowsy. Stress over sleep makes sleep impossible. Finally, get regular exercise. Nothing is better for helping encourage your body to rest.

Diet. Exercise. Rest. I realize you probably didn't open this book to be nagged about these common responsibilities, and I also know I haven't told you anything you didn't already know. But if you're reading this line, I'm pleased that you didn't skip this section! I simply can't overstate how critical these areas of personal maintenance are for you.

I suggest that today is a very good time to sit down with a sheet of paper and take a personal inventory of what you eat, what physical activity you pursue, and how regularly you rest. Write down the true facts: What meals have you eaten during the last three days? Have you adequately represented the food groups? Are you taking appropriate vitamins or getting them in your diet? What about exercise? If you don't have a current plan, are you willing to start one? Who will exercise with you and hold you accountable? I strongly recommend that you avoid exercising alone, because it is too easy to get out of the habit. And what about sleep? Diet, exercise, and routine are the places to begin for that one, but you also need to think about your emotional health at present. Let's take a moment to consider that.

CARE FOR YOUR EMOTIONS

How is your stress level these days? Stress is defined medically as your physiological response to an external stimulus. The appearance of any kind of threat (including a simple threat to our happiness) triggers what is known as the fight-or-flight reaction. In other words, a mosquito lands on your arm, and your decision is probably to fight, by swatting it. But if a car comes racing down a street you happen to be crossing, then flight is your immediate choice— you'd be crazy to fight a fast car!

When we are faced with the mystery of the unexpected, we're not certain how we should respond or what we should do. Mind, body, and spirit are thrown into some level of turmoil, and this is what we call stress. We feel anxiety, fear, perhaps anger and other emotions. In the situation this book addresses, there can be fear in several quarters. If you're having problems relating to your adult child, you and your son or daughter both feel negative stress—which, by the way, is known as *distress*. Positive stress, which we rarely discuss, is known as *eustress*. You might feel that the week you're getting married or preparing for a trip overseas.

> If you're having problems relating to your adult child, you and your son or daughter both feel negative stress.

If your twenty-something is living at home, asking for money, arguing with you about his lifestyle or something along those lines, you are facing the probability of turbulent emotions. These might include anger, accompanied by arguments and bitterness; sorrow and depression; worry and anxiety; perhaps even an almost bipolar roller-coaster experience of relief and disappointment as you struggle to see the problems right themselves. Intense emotions can tire us out more than we realize. We can end up feeling drained and empty, and we'll be likely to suffer from some degree of depression.

What can you do? The solution would be easy if the problems were easy, but in most cases they're not. If you've hit a rough spot in relating to your twenty-something, you're simply not certain how it's all going to end up. Therefore, you have to decide that your inner strength will not be based on the desirability of the circumstances. Is that possible? Yes. Easy? No.

Being emotionally resilient requires you to confront and manage your own feelings. We've already talked a bit about anger, the most important of these feelings. If you're not careful, and you don't tend the home fires, your anger will quietly build, even as you stifle the expressions of it. You will find, as all of this anger is bottled up within you, that occasionally the anger is going to come out in an unpleasant and irrational form. Therefore, you need to know exactly

> Being emotionally resilient requires you to confront and manage your own feelings.

how you feel about all that is going on in your life. You have to stop and take time simply for yourself, forgetting for at least an hour or two about your child, your spouse, your many responsibilities, and all the rest. Perhaps you need to take a break and go away for a day to somewhere you won't be disturbed so that you can sort through the current events of your life.

There will have to be people who can help you deal with these feelings. If you don't have a spouse who is a good listener, then you will have to find someone else—a close friend at church, among your siblings, or in your neighborhood. Work on expressing your frustrations verbally and pleasantly, as explained earlier in the book. You'll be managing your anger maturely, and you'll feel a good bit better.

I always recommend keeping a journal of your emotions as well. Talk as much as you can with an intimate acquaintance, but there are still going to be some things that are kept between you and God. As a matter of fact, you might want to keep this diary in the form of a prayer journal. We'll talk about the spiritual element in the next section.

When you feel overcome by your circumstances, stop and take a few moments alone. Practice slow, deep breathing to normalize your heart rate and respiration. Take a brisk walk as soon as possible. Be certain you're eating right and getting enough rest. Avoid nicotine, caffeine, alcohol, and other stimulants. And try practicing positive self-talk. Tell yourself things such as, "This is difficult for me, and I'm struggling with my feelings about this situation. But God gave me strength, he gave me good friends, and I'm going to hang tough. I will respond in love and wisdom rather than reacting in a knee-jerk way. I insist that life is going to get better!"

What about medication? Some Christians believe that it's somehow unspiritual or worldly to use medication. That's about as true as if a diabetic decided not to take insulin for the same reasons—or a teenager with a broken leg decided not to wear a cast. Share your feelings with a doctor or perhaps even a qualified family counselor. There's a possibility that an antidepressant will be prescribed, and it could be a great help to you by balancing out the artificial highs and lows of your daily emotions. You should also see that your child has good medical advice and considers the same options.

CARE FOR YOUR SPIRIT

The root *psych* in psychology is taken from the Greek word for *soul*. Yes, we are spiritual creatures. We are more than our bodies and even our thoughts and feelings. Christians believe that we were created to be God's children, and deep inside, we know we are eternal, immortal creatures who realize that life, as God intended it, should be much better.

When things go wrong, many people immediately look to heaven and say, "Why me, God?" The better question, of course, is "Why not me?" Trouble is the domain of all people. It has been that way since the beginning. Who among us believes we should be the ones favored to lead lives free of any pain, when so many people have suffered more deeply? We could ask "Why me?" about all the good things God has bestowed—life, health, the joy of having children, the state of living in a time and a place where we enjoy freedom and prosperity—but somehow we don't think to question our worthiness for so many good things.

Why am I sharing these philosophical ruminations with you in a book about parenting adult children? Because your spiritual perspective is so important during a crisis. So many of us have trusted God in the tough times, and as a result we have become stronger and wiser. We don't know why there is so much pain in life, but we do know that God uses it to make us better people. And we don't always know why a twenty-five-year-old adult would act like a child, but we do know that his mistakes are going to teach him maturity better than any sermons we can preach.

Please don't let your anxiety close you off from God. What a tragic mistake, when he is the greatest resource we can possibly imagine for trying times. Dig deeper into your prayer life and your study of the Bible. I strongly recommend the Psalms during a particularly challenging season of life; the psalmists give us a good model of really being honest with God, daring to shake our fists at the heavens when we are frustrated. God is big enough to handle our honesty. You're not going to hurt his feelings. As a matter of fact, seek him more intimately during this time, and you'll surely find him.

I also hope you have a good church to attend during these times—a church that provides you with a good support group of encouragers and comforters. In the next section, we'll talk about the wonderful role these people can play during a tough time.

CARE FROM YOUR COMMUNITY

I notice how often adults fail to ask for help. Why is it that some great challenge causes us to cloister ourselves, cutting us off from the assistance we need and that others are so willing to offer?

Let me give you an example. In the story that opens this chapter, Joan in particular is struggling with full-time grandparenting. She is chasing a four-year-old around the house and changing the diapers of a twelve-month-old. This important responsibility was never anticipated; it came in the middle of the night, and it has changed her life.

> Pride reaps a terrible price in our lives when we don't ask for help.

Jim and Joan are churchgoers, but they've said very little about the whole affair to the friends in their Sunday school class. Part of their reticence, frankly, is their embarrassment over what has happened to their son, Jason. They had bragged so much about his wife and his family, and now they'd rather avoid the subject.

Yet within their circle of close friends are several empty nesters with time on their hands—one or two single women in particular who absolutely love being around children. If Joan were to ask one of them to help her on Tuesday, and the other on Thursday, both women would be delighted. As a matter of fact, it would be a ministry not only from them but to them, because they are lonely and need to give and receive love.

> We are a bit older, we get tired a little quicker, but there's strength in numbers.

Every one of us knows people who would rise to the challenge if they knew we would let them help. Pride reaps a terrible price in our lives when we don't ask for help—or perhaps we simply haven't thought it through. There are other options for us to consider, depending on our situation, if we simply use our minds. Martyrdom isn't always a necessity!

Particularly in the case of grandparents, I want to emphasize this point: we are a bit older, we get tired a little quicker, but there's strength in numbers. We need to help one another out, and I believe a great many of us are willing to do so. Your friends are an untapped resource, a treasure yet to be claimed.

ARE YOU UP TO THE TASK?

Finally, I'm going to ask you a very important question. And it's not one to be shrugged away or scoffed at.

Can you handle the situation you're confronted with?

It applies to any situation you are facing with your twenty-something, but I'm speaking particularly, in this case, to the situation we've just touched on: grandparents who are suddenly faced with the necessity of parenting their children's children full-time. This is a trend all over our nation, as marriages struggle and grandparents are called in to help. Visit nearly any church today, and you'll find several instances of Grandma and Grandpa with a child or two in tow who are a little too young to be theirs.

The problem is that when these situations arise, we believe we have no choice. It seems to be an emergency, and again, what mother or father could look at the tearstained face of their adult child and say no? They appear on our doorsteps brokenhearted, and we absolutely can't turn them away.

> Grandchildren require constant love and affection, a positive attitude, a certain level of energy, and plenty of planning.

At least not for a week or two. But I challenge you to answer the question of this section. Are you up to the task? Because if you're not, what are the consequences? If you try to do what you're not in condition to do, it will wreak havoc on your life. Therefore, I suggest that there may be more options than you think. Certainly, if you can help, then you should do so within reason. If you cannot, then you need to sit down with your adult child and come up with plan B or plan C, keeping in mind that the ultimate responsibility for these grandchildren is not yours but your son's or daughter's.

Remember this: those grandchildren require constant love and affection, a positive attitude, a certain level of energy, and plenty of planning. Yes, you definitely have the experience to raise them, but you must count the full cost. If you come to the serious conclusion that you don't have the health or the stamina to do what needs to be done, then the *loving* thing, not only for yourself but for your child and grandchildren, is to explain why you can't give all the assistance that you would like. If you run yourself down until you are in poor health, then your child's problem will be even greater.

So think it through. If you have a healthy self-love, you'll care for your body, your mind, and your soul more now than ever. And when you have done that to the best of your ability, you'll be able to take a closer look at those very needs in the life of your adult child. That's the subject of our next chapter.

{six}

MIND, MOOD, AND MEDS

Imagine you and I are having a pleasant chat over a cup of coffee. I ask you to tell me about your adult child. What are the first five or six sentences of description you are likely to offer me?

I predict you will talk about the general circumstances of your twenty-something's life. You might tell me her age and whether or not she is living at home. You will tell me about her job if she has one, or whether she is a student, and what her plans may be.

We think of the years just after the twentieth birthday as a time of action and achievement, don't we? This is the all-important launch phase for the mission that is her life. As you've raised her from infancy, childhood, and on through adolescence, you have wondered what she is going to *do* with her life; whom she will marry, whether she will have a career, and how many children she will raise.

We've been waiting a long time for the answers, and if there's a delay (as there is with so many in this age-group today), we become even more focused on those circumstances. *When* will she decide? *Where* is she going to live? *How* is she going to get there? And so on. The great danger is that if we look so closely at what's on the outside, we fail to consider the vital importance of what's going on inside the adult child. If you'll think about it for a moment, you'll realize that the great majority of our actions are determined by our thoughts and emotions.

In the previous chapter, I sought to help you think about the significance of your own wellness—mind, body, and spirit—in doing the job of parenting. In this chapter, we'll look at some of those same issues. But now we're talking about how to evaluate the mental, physical, and spiritual health of your twenty-something child. If her life seems stuck in neutral, why is that so? If she has struggled with a romantic relationship, how has that affected her spirit? How well do you really know this young adult for whom you have sacrificed, labored, and given your best for two decades?

During the last half century we've seen a revolution in our understanding of the physiology of the human personality. We've come to understand emotions with much more clarity and depth, and we've begun to see just how biology impacts psychology—and vice versa. There have been great strides in achieving a holistic understanding of who we are and why we act as we do. Those of us who are people of faith balance the newer learning with the ancient wisdom. We believe that all truth is God's truth, and that our understanding of the soul is enhanced by what we are learning about the body and the mind.

> If we look so closely at what's on the outside, we fail to consider the vital importance of what's going on inside the adult child.

In particular, there are several trends that seem to have great prominence in the lives of younger people today, up to and including this generation under thirty years old. What do you need to know about some of these phenomena? How can you support your adult child and, when necessary, get her the care she needs? Let's explore some considerations about the health and wellness of your child in light of recent developments and trends.

"QUARTERLIFE CRISIS"

Are you ready for another "trend label"? How about "quarterlife crisis"? It's the latest developmental buzzword to describe what magazine writers and social observers are seeing.

In this particular model of the young adult experience, twenty-somethings eagerly enter the job world then find themselves dissatisfied with the rat race. They drop out and regroup to consider the next strategy, possibly by moving back home to think it through.

"Many young Americans feel anxiety when faced with a wide range of opportunities in their twenties and are unsure of how to choose from among them," says Dr. Jeffrey Arnett, the doctor who has promoted the idea of emerging adulthood. "They have grown up as the most affluent generation in American history, so they have high expectations for life. They all expect to find a job that not only pays well, but is enjoyable, and they all expect to find their 'soul mate.'"[1]

Is this scenario being overhyped? The Web page www.quarterlifecrisis.com receives one million hits per month from ten thousand registered users who log on for advice and to compare notes in their search for a passionate pursuit and a mate to pursue it with. Abby Wilner, who operates the Web site and has authored a book called *The Quarterlifer's Companion*, cites these imposing statistics:

- Half of all students graduate with college debt, which averages $12,000, according to the American Council of Education.

- Nearly two-thirds of young adults in their early twenties receive economic support from their parents, while 40 percent still receive assistance in their late twenties, according to the American Sociological Association.

- The average American age eighteen to thirty has held seven to eight different jobs, according to the U.S. Census.

- According to the Census Bureau's Current Population Survey, 56.8 percent of men and 43.2 percent of women twenty-two to thirty-one years old lived at home with their parents or planned to move back home after graduation in 2002.[2]

It's difficult to argue with the conclusion that our country is now more than ever filled with people in this age-group who feel they're in a bind. We've discussed all the reasons for this elsewhere. The important questions are: How is this enigma affecting our children, and how can we help them get past the barriers they're facing?

The most obvious answer to the first question is that many of our adult children are experiencing deep anxiety. Listen to the words of one twenty-something:

I often say to my friends that I think there are two paths in our twenties that we are very concerned about. One is career and one is falling in love, and I think what it all has to do with is avoiding a feeling of loneliness. A part of me wants to have a path. And I sometimes worry—I think that I've been trying to work really hard the past couple of years on being okay with not having a path, but every time I would begin to allow myself to feel that, there was a part of me that went, "You have to have a path." It's also a lot about feeling trapped. I worry sometimes that I'll never feel like I've arrived, that I'll always have inner turmoil.[3]

You can certainly feel the levels of stress and anxiety in that statement, and I believe the speaker is very perceptive in identifying loneliness as a major factor. Let's think for a moment about anxiety and the twenty-something.

ANXIETY

Anxiety is an intense combination of negative emotions that include fear, apprehension, and worry. It affects the mind and the body as well as the feelings. An estimated 15 percent of Americans suffer from some anxiety disorder such as generalized anxiety, phobias, obsessive-compulsive disorder, or frequent and unexpected panic attacks.[4] Most common of all is that quiet but ever-present anxiety that life simply isn't what it's supposed to be; that some of the puzzle pieces are missing, and we aren't where we expected to be by this time.

For your adult child, the great source of anxiety is probably a fear of the future. It might revolve around "having no path," as the young adult phrased it, or of not knowing which of several paths to choose. In the other great issue, that of marriage and a mate, the anxiety could be about the dangers of either making a great mistake or even finding no one at all. There is the fear of failure that we all feel as we come right to the edge of the diving board in the swimming pool of life: *What if I miss? What if I hurt myself? How do I really know I'm not destined for failure?*

We often talk about stress when we discuss anxiety. We defined stress in the last chapter as your whole-body response to significant change. In the case of a twenty-something child moving home, could it be that your central issue is stress while your child's great challenge is anxiety? You are coping with what is happening in your life, and your child is coping with what is *not* happening in her life. Your life is established, but your child has great worries about the future. And she cannot see through the fog to determine what lies in that future for her life.

Is anxiety all bad? No. Like stress, it has a good form. Your child *should* be anxious about the future; she should be actively engaged in laying the foundation for it, as we all are. Manageable anxiety motivates us to get to work, to prepare for the important responsibilities as they arise. It helps us study for a test, clean the house before company comes, or get our taxes prepared in time. Your task is to help your young adult manage the normal anxiety that comes with a huge transition point in life. To some extent we manage anxiety as we do anger. We don't suppress it by "putting on a happy face" and denying that it's there, but we express it verbally and pleasantly.

> You are coping with what is happening in your life, and your child is coping with what is not happening in her life.

A little boy in an old comic strip had an "anxiety closet." Inside it lurked one thousand vague worries about the future, and when the light went out at bedtime, he worried about all the unseen anxieties in the closet. It's an apt metaphor for the worry that disables many of us and many of our children. What's helpful about that word picture is the prompting to consider that anxieties can be very subjective. They can take on much greater power over us when they're kept in the dark. We shed light on them by bringing them out into the open, discussing them with our loved ones.

Can you help your adult child do this without it becoming either a nag-fest or an altercation? We dealt with some guidelines for loving discussion in the third chapter. For present purposes, allow me to emphasize that your listening skills will be more crucial than ever during this period of time.

It may be a challenge to keep your own frustration and impatience from becoming an obstacle to communicating with your adult child. Just remember that what she needs during this period of time is an improved ability to think about her life, the world, and the future. Try to put yourself in your child's shoes and see the great question mark that is our world from her perspective. You want her to succeed; she wants that too. She wants to find that pathway to success very carefully, avoiding the career that is dull and depersonalizing and steering clear of the marriage that crashes and creates suffering. The key is to help her verbalize the challenges before her, the emotions she feels about those challenges, and what process of decision making she is going to use.

> Try to put yourself in your child's shoes and see the great question mark that is our world from her perspective.

One strategy is to help her see in terms of the factors she can control and those she cannot. Is it possible to have absolute knowledge about whether a particular career will bring satisfaction? No, we have to step out in faith to some degree. Is it possible to gain information, to learn as much as possible about our own aptitudes, to thoroughly investigate the existing job options, and to make the most rational possible decision based on the evidence? Yes, absolutely. And in showing how to work through this kind of logical, real-world thinking, you will help your adult child reason in an effective and mature manner. That's one of the best weapons against anxiety that I know about: careful reason and proactive planning.

This will also be an opportunity to help train your young adult child to think *spiritually* about the problems of life. Here is a passage from the New Testament that always provides powerful encouragement during a time of worry and stress:

> Do not be anxious about anything, but in everything, by prayer and petition, with thanksgiving, present your requests to God. And the peace of God, which transcends all understanding, will guard your hearts and your minds in Christ Jesus. (Phil. 4:6–7)

In those words we hear the apostle Paul saying that no problem is so large that God isn't larger still. Are we worried about the future? God knows every detail of it. He has plans for each one of us, and they are plans that will make us happy because he loves us. We simply need to gather up all those anxieties. We can bring them out of that dark closet, take their accurate measure in the light, and hand them over to the Lord's care.

> God's peace, so profound and deep that we cannot comprehend it, will guard our hearts and our minds.

Can we know we'll be free of problems and unpleasantness? Not at all. But Paul promises that God's peace, so profound and deep that we cannot comprehend it, will guard our hearts and our minds. Those are more than bland words of positive thinking. I believe they describe the genuine, living presence of God in our lives as we trust him.

Can you talk to your adult child about how God has given you that kind of peace? Can you use examples from your own early adult experience, telling how uncertain the world looked for you at one time?

From the beginning of her life, your child came to you when she was anxious, perhaps when she was afraid of the dark or worried about school. You are still her voice of comfort and strength, and God will give you the right words to help your twenty-something deal with the new and pressing anxieties of facing the adult world.

DEPRESSION

Related to the negative emotions associated with anxiety, we see an unsettling increase in reported cases of depression among our young people. Ronald Kessler of Harvard Medical School studied eight thousand Americans ages fifteen to fifty-four. Of those now forty-five to fifty-four, only 2 percent reported symptoms of depression by their late teens. But in the age range of fifteen to twenty-four, 23 percent reported serious depression before age twenty.[5] It seems clear that depression is either more prevalent than in the past or we are simply much more aware of it at younger ages.

We need to clarify our terms carefully. There is situational depression, which is common to nearly all people. It comes and goes with the ups and downs of life. However, when a depressed mood lingers for more than two weeks and is accompanied by other symptoms that interfere with daily living, it could be a case of clinical depression. If your adult child has hit a rough stage in life and feels helpless or frustrated in her attempts to work through it, then she could be a candidate for a bout with depression. Emotional reactions to negative developments in life are probably the most common triggers for this pervasive problem.

Various studies show that about one in six people will cope with clinical depression at some time in life, and the twenties are the average or typical period of time when it happens. Women seem to be twice as likely to suffer from depression (or perhaps to report the problem).

One problem in recognizing depression in a young adult is that she can hide it very well. Some have called this camouflaged problem "smiling depression," because younger people are concerned about how they appear, and they'll take greater pains to disguise their emotions. However, the mask is most often applied in public situations—among the young adult's friends. You as the parent have an opportunity to see your adult child when she is more likely to be herself, bad moods and all. How can you recognize depression and distinguish it from simple and temporarily low spirits? Look for not one but several of these signs:

> One in six people will cope with clinical depression at some time in life, and the twenties are the average or typical period of time when it happens.

- Subdued mood
- Loss of pleasure in normal activities
- Excessive sadness
- Extremes: eating too little or too much

- Extremes: sleeping too little or too much
- Emotions: guilt, helplessness, hopelessness, anxiety, fear
- An inability to make decisions
- Regular thoughts about death

Note that any individual item in that list, taken by itself, would be rather common and insignificant. When you see several of these behaviors together for an extended period of time, however, you should consult a physician or qualified counselor about the possibility of your child suffering from depression. The least likely person to recognize the presence of the disorder is the young adult who suffers from it, so please realize that your child is likely to resist your concerns and your desire to have her examined.

Clinical depression is a serious problem that can render the sufferer almost incapable of living an active and healthy life. It will sabotage her chances of getting off to a good start in the work world and building a family of her own. If your adult child has come home to live, it could be that she has done so because she unconsciously realizes that something is wrong with her inside. Maybe she knows that she can't adequately care for herself at present. So watch carefully, as a loving parent always does, and be aware of the signs that are obvious as well as those that are subtle.

BIPOLAR DISORDER

During the early years of my career in counseling, one seldom encountered bipolar disorder. Now, unfortunately, it is a frequent and significant force in the emotional challenges of our world. When we speak of bipolar disorder, we think most commonly of the unpredictability of extreme mood swings, from highly energized to subdued and sad. Mood, energy, sleep, activities, and even thinking are all at the mercy of these alternating shifts.

Again, we need to be wary of the dangers of amateur diagnosis. But you can at least raise the question of this problem to a physician if you notice that your adult child can alternately be vibrant, excited, and on top of the world, then suddenly depressed, withdrawn, and incapable of functioning normally. If your child experienced high levels of anxiety or depression in younger years, she is more likely to be a candidate for bipolar disorder.

> If your child experienced high levels of anxiety or depression in younger years, she is more likely to be a candidate for bipolar disorder.

When we speak of this severe kind of disorder, of course, we have crossed into an area where you will definitely need to consult a good physician who will help you and your adult child take steps toward emotional health. There are many promising new medications and treatment methods for this and other forms of clinical depression.

ADHD

Attention-deficit/hyperactivity disorder has become a popular topic in our time. Many children are being treated for symptoms of this problem, but some people don't realize that it is an adult problem as well. As a matter of fact, in two-thirds of the cases of childhood ADHD, the symptoms persist into adulthood. Has your adult child been diagnosed with this condition?

ADHD is a wide-ranging and only partially understood phenomenon that affects attention span, impulsivity, coordination, and many other normal facets of daily living. It is closely associated with anxiety, depression, substance abuse, and other problems, so we must take it seriously.

The classic ADHD behavior, of course, is the inability to concentrate in one direction for an extended period of time. ADHD sufferers often struggle in the classroom for that reason; they can be very intelligent, yet seemingly unable to get good grades. They can be fidgety in church during the sermon, and they are always switching radio or television stations. They are people who need constant stimulation of the senses, and when they do find an object of special interest—an art project or an absorbing book—they "hyperfocus," and their attention to the task is focused with laser intensity.

> Every adult who suffers from ADHD shows symptoms of the disorder in a different way, and must be treated accordingly.

The study of ADHD is controversial, as you may have noticed. A great deal of argument continues over whether it even exists, how it should be treated, and so on. Be discerning as you read and study to get more information on ADHD, because there are many misleading things being said about it. There is also a problem in that every adult who suffers from ADHD shows symptoms of the disorder in a different way and must be treated accordingly. Some have no problems with attention span but happen to be very impulsive. Others manifest their symptoms in completely different directions.

The good news is that medication has been highly successful in dealing with the symptoms of ADHD. There are also lifestyle adjustments that can be made to help people with this disorder live quite normal and successful daily lives. As a matter of fact, those diagnosed with ADHD very often possess some great talent or ability. Artists and highly intelligent thinkers and leaders make up the ranks of the ADHD world.

So there's certainly no reason to worry too greatly about being diagnosed with this disorder; we simply need to treat it and to learn what adjustments can be made in life so that it doesn't become an impediment. It's clear that an extreme case of ADHD can become an obstacle in your young adult child's ability to work at her job or function within a personal relationship. Yet diagnosis and treatment can help you and her realize the special areas and gifts of her personality and use them to her (and her world's) advantage rather than disadvantage.

SUBSTANCE ABUSE

Drugs and alcohol are often a tremendous problem for young adults. Certainly this generation (like past ones) has used mood alteration as a way to cope with fear, anxiety, or unhappiness. We're also reaping what we have sown as a pleasure-driven culture: our world is blanketed with advertisements and endorsements of the "highs" that can be attained in life.

Sex, drugs, alcohol, and every other sensual source are to be squeezed for every last drop of temporary thrills.

> We're reaping what we have sown as a pleasure-driven culture.

At the same time, social life for young adults too often seems to revolve around bars and excessive drinking. It's sad to realize that the church has really struggled to respond to this need; it has failed in general to draw in the younger generations. As a result, there are seldom any wholesome Christian social events that a typical twenty-something adult would consider attending. Many young adults aren't necessarily seeking a lifestyle built around drinking, but they drift into one as they search for friendships (romantic and otherwise) with people their age. Peer pressure in the twenties is not much different from peer pressure among teenagers. If everyone else in the room has a glass of scotch or bourbon, then the newcomer, who wants to fit in comfortably, will feel pulled toward imitating that behavior.

The issue of self-esteem enters the conversation here. Young adults will struggle in this area if they are finding it difficult to get their lives moving. They are much more likely to turn to the quick stimulation of drugs and alcohol either for emotional escape or to simply fit in with the young adult world as they find it.

If you notice your child drawing closer to the problem of substance abuse, her self-esteem could be an area worthy of your consideration. Again, if your love is constant, powerful, and unconditional, this is less likely to be a problem. A young adult with a strong self-concept is less likely to feel the need to conform to the behavior of others. Help her work on that self-image, and keep the channels of communication open.

Don't be slow to confront the problem of chemical addiction. It can ruin a life as nothing else can. It will destroy relationships, damage careers, and endanger the lives of others, particularly when automobiles are involved. If you discover this problem in your family, you will want to seek counseling immediately. There is likely to be a problem in getting cooperation from the one with the dependency; drug and alcohol abusers can be very insistent in their denial. They are afraid to face the reality that their lives are out of control, and they are afraid of the physical process and the pain of the adjustment in becoming completely sober.

You may need help through an organized intervention. You will also need a great deal of prayer to God and tough, stubborn love for your child.

MATERIALISM

Another area in which we're reaping what we've sown is that of rampant consumerism. This may seem like a surprising category for this chapter, but it's an important consideration in discussing the welfare of your young adult child. Beware, because it may also touch a nerve in your own life.

No one would argue that we live in a materialistic, consumer-driven culture. Madison Avenue, world capital of the advertising industry, has become totally dominant. Many of us believe that we really do need the latest and greatest version of the device known as the television. We "need" bigger screens, high-definition pictures, and home theater sound. And who wants to drive an older model car if we can afford better?

> We must look at the materialism of our children and realize that we probably had a great deal to do with it.

It's been sad for me to notice how many parents can't afford to pay for the educational needs of their children simply because they are in so much debt for the large house they felt was essential, the beach home, and whatever else they have sunk their funds into. It's not that they don't love their children, but they're certainly not modeling the concept of wise and loving financial management.

Therefore, if we are honest, we must look at the materialism of our children and realize that we probably had a great deal to do with it. If we are to help them understand the fallacy of this philosophy, we'll need to set the pace ourselves.

The important thing is to realize, and to help our children realize, that the dream of finding happiness through the expenditure of money is always an illusion. We know that fact objectively, but our lives testify otherwise. Are we really any happier than we were with the possessions we had twenty or thirty years ago? Would a mansion guarantee a contented state of mind? Unfortunately, many young adults believe so. To a large extent, they are in a hurry not just to earn an income but to earn a *fortune*. This is one reason that some of them can't seem to move forward in their twenties—they want the most lucrative and satisfying career so badly that they're not willing to start in the mail room and work their way up.

In fairness, it's also true that there are many twenty-somethings who are strikingly different from the materialistic picture I've painted above. As I'll demonstrate in Chapter 8, some of them are driven much more by personal passion than by salary. They want the job that is inspired by their most cherished personal interest, even if they can't live on the pay that it brings. At the same time, we see a great number of young people entering the military, the Peace Corps, and various kinds of mission work. Armies of twenty-somethings converged on the Gulf Coast after the devastation of Hurricane Katrina.

So we don't want to paint this entire generation with one broad and negative brush. There is also great hope and reason to be excited about many trends with this group. We do have to recognize that there is a problem with rampant consumerism, just as there has been in the American generations that preceded it. If you note this problem in your young adult child, there isn't a simple cure or a medication that will address it. The treatment, of course, is purely a spiritual one. And we'll devote a chapter to that one near the end of this book.

A FEW WORDS ABOUT MEDICATION AND HEALTH COVERAGE

Jessica Cullen, twenty-three, was one of those young people with high ideals. After graduating from college, she moved to Charlotte, North Carolina, to begin a career in fund-raising. She wanted to help charities and nonprofit agencies raise money. She was happy with her job, though it offered only $1,600 monthly before tax, and no health benefits. She did briefly shop around for cut-rate health plans, but $80 per month seemed to be the cost, and that was more than she could produce on such a salary.

Her parents' group coverage helped out for six months, but after that she had been out of college too long for the policy to apply. So Jessica found herself without any medical coverage.[6] And she's not alone. Nearly one in three young adults between the ages of eighteen and twenty-four live without health insurance—the highest proportion of any age-group, according to the U.S. Census Bureau. Between ages twenty-five and thirty-four, it's one in four adults. That's the second-largest uninsured group.[7]

> Twenty-somethings are the least likely age-group to enjoy the benefits of health coverage.

Therefore, we conclude that twenty-somethings are the least likely age-group to enjoy the benefits of health coverage. At this age, of course, many of them feel invulnerable; they're in the peak of health and rarely see a doctor, so why should they worry? But if Jessica had an automobile accident, became gravely ill, or was diagnosed with a disorder that required medication, she would be helpless to pay for the care she needed.

There is an important reason your young adult child should not gamble on her youthful good health. If she develops a medical condition of any kind, it will be too late to act. Short-term insurance won't cover preexisting conditions. It makes much more sense to invest in limited coverage now, even if it's only a short-term plan. I'm telling this to you, the parent, because your adult child is less likely to be concerned about the medical coverage she doesn't expect to need. If you want to help your child out financially, this is the best and most loving option you could choose.

Prescription-drug coverage, unfortunately, is a particularly expensive part of any insurance policy. It could add as much as $50 per month. But again, it's cheaper to arrange for that coverage now, before the need for it is discovered. The good news is that an individual plan offers lower rates to a young and healthy applicant; group policies apply the same rates regardless of age or status.

Medication has become an important issue for so many of us. It's not unusual for ordinary people to take several prescription drugs—perhaps for allergies, for depression, or for some other very common need. Has your child had a complete physical examination lately? Are you sure she has whatever medication she may need? As we saw in the previous chapter, your adult child will be at her best if she attends to her physical, emotional, and spiritual needs. And there are many ways you can help her do that.

In the next few chapters of this book, we'll talk about some very specific needs: financial, work-related, social, and spiritual.

seven

CASH, CREDIT,
AND CHARACTER

Jane Goodall, the British anthropologist, studied chimpanzees in their native African habitat over a period of four decades. She told the story of Flo, a mother chimp, and the son named Flint who was born to Flo in her later years. Yes, we're talking about chimpanzees. But the story offers an apt metaphor of what can also happen in human families.

Goodall writes that Flo was an exceptional mother who was affectionate and playful. She was also highly respected in her community and an aggressive leader. But the time came when Flo began to slow down a bit. She showed a marked decrease in the energy and leadership that had once been hers. Meanwhile, Flint, at four years old, had somehow become a spoiled child within his extended and overly tolerant family. It was time for him to be weaned and to begin showing evidence of adult chimpanzee behavior. But it wasn't happening. Flint continued to ride on his tired mother's back, and he preferred his mother's milk to finding his own food.

When Flo tried to wean her growing son, Flint would throw violent tantrums. He would even bite or strike his mother—rare behavior among chimpanzees.

Flo was simply too tired to stand firm, and in time she found it easier to simply give in. She couldn't even get him to leave the nest that was supposed to be a home for the younger children only. Flint was stubborn, defiant, and strong, and he remained around his mother until she passed away.

So what did Flint do next? His mother's death left him in shock; he had not learned autonomy and independence. Instead he retreated into a sullen isolation, refusing to eat or to interact with the larger chimp community. He could not or would not care for himself, and it finally cost him his life.[1]

I have seen the human version of this scenario played out many times. If a child becomes like Peter Pan and won't grow up, his only destination is Neverland. He will never learn to care for himself; he will never be able to stand on his own two feet. For the parents, it seems so much easier to simply give in—not only easier, but often something we desire unconsciously. Most of the time we enjoy having our children living around us. If we have a few extra resources, a spare bedroom, and a little bit of spare time, why not let our child share it all with us? We're a family, after all, and we don't want to think that our children are leaving us.

> Our first responsibility as parents is to prepare our children to replace us in this world by cutting the apron strings and building adult lives of their own.

Seductive as that reasoning can be, the problem is that our first responsibility as parents is to prepare our children to replace us in this world by cutting the apron strings and building adult lives of their own. Listen to the beautiful words of the psalmist:

Sons are a heritage from the Lord,
    children a reward from him.
Like arrows in the hands of a warrior
    are sons born in one's youth.
Blessed is the man
    whose quiver is full of them. (Ps. 127:3–5)

Place yourself in that word picture. As a mother or father, you are the warrior standing on the battlefront, your eyes on the horizon. You reach for another arrow from your quiver and fire it high into the clouds, where it vanishes before completing its graceful arc. It is ours to release those wonderful arrows called children toward heaven; they finally soar we know not where, for God guides the arc of their journey from the moment they leave our loving and protective hands.

> What will happen to them when we are no longer here to solve all their problems?

The difference between children and arrows is that the arrows don't try to climb back into the quiver. The archer doesn't become attached to his missiles.

As our children grow older, we need to remember at every moment that we are still preparing them to live without us. What will happen to them when we are no longer here to solve all their problems? How much discipline and autonomy will they have learned? Will they go forward and change the world positively, or will they grow sullen, as Flint did, and begin withering away?

While that's really the theme of this entire book, I believe that no issue crystallizes the point like that of money. Finance is certainly the practical center of our world today, and in a way it becomes the proving ground of how well we have trained our children.

> Finance is certainly the practical center of our world today, and in a way it becomes the proving ground of how well we have trained our children.

There are two basic components to this chapter. The first involves how to handle the issue of your own money as it relates to your children and their support; the second involves how to help your adult child manage his own money in a time when it can become the make-or-break issue for twenty-somethings. I hope you'll find a great deal of practical guidance in the following pages.

MONEY AND RESPONSIBILITY

Let's speak first about an issue that has unfortunately become a primary theme among parents and their adult children these days. It has to do with the ability of twenty-somethings to manipulate their parents into giving them the resources they desire. Let me point out quickly that I realize the young adults usually don't comprehend that they're doing this. They are focused on what they need, they haven't learned how to earn it on their own, and they know exactly how to press the buttons that cause Mom or Dad to come through for them.

Parents tend to be farther along in life and financially established, with at least a little bit of cash reserve. Their children, of course, have yet to get a solid footing in the career world. They may already possess a great deal of debt through college loans. Much more than that, they may possess a taste for the same luxuries and privileges with which they have grown up, and they may be impatient to reach the lifestyle goals they've unrealistically set.

Many of us were raised simply, and it wasn't so unthinkable to start out our own adult lives simply, with the bare necessities. The question is more difficult for a consumer generation that has come of age with more expensive tastes. And of course, we want the best for our children; we enjoy giving them gifts. We don't want them to be unhappy, and sometimes we continue providing them with cars, cash allowances,

> He would have made every decision much differently if he knew it was all completely up to him and that he would suffer the consequences of failure to work and to pay.

and other things during the time when they frankly need to be learning the disciplines of finance and the virtue of earning the things they receive.

All of these factors set the stage for the problem. Like Flint the chimpanzee, the adult child continues in dependence too long. He approaches Mom and Dad and asks for a few extra bucks. Perhaps he wants them to make the down payment on a shiny new car he has spotted. "I'm going to be working," he says persuasively. "I'll make all the monthly payments, if you'll just put the initial money down." It seems like a small thing, and we are certain that he understands his own responsibilities.

But several months later, it's clear that he must give up on that job possibility in which he has placed so much hope. He is in limbo now, networking and checking the want ads. "By the way,

I'm behind on my car payments, Dad," he says. "I was wondering if you could help me for a couple of months."

Part of the reason we have this situation is that the son knew all along that if worse came to worse, he didn't absolutely have to make every car payment; Dad would be there for him. He didn't have to make that first job work; his parents were his safety net. He would have made every decision much differently if he knew it was all completely up to him and that he would suffer the consequences of failure to work and to pay.

In other words, he has not learned the discipline that comes from knowing he must absolutely stand on his own two feet. This is a very difficult lesson for parents to teach, and my heart goes out to them. It's difficult to say no sometimes; we want to see our children smile, and we want to hear them say, "Mom, Dad, you're the best!" But in the long run, being too permissive is unfair to our children. Much more than we owe them a sports car, a new laptop computer, or a nice apartment, we owe them the legacy of learning to live as responsible adults.

Take as an example some particular responsibility that your child presently has. It could be paying off his college loan, or it could be the charges on his brand-new credit card. I have always maintained that two people cannot share one responsibility. If your child knows that you will always save the day, and that no unpleasant consequences can come to him, then it is not his responsibility—it has become yours. One of you has to bear the burden. If he doesn't bear this one, when will he learn? If you begin intercepting his bills because you're afraid he'll simply ignore them and ruin his credit, then again, you have become responsible for his credit line.

There's no easy or anxiety-free way to approach this task. He must bear responsibility, and he must bear it alone, or he will never bear any at all.

MONEY AND MANIPULATION

In the most regrettable cases, parents get the idea that if they just give their children enough money, then everything will work out. We tend to think this because we fix other problems with money: a dented fender, an outdated living room design. Money is what we have at this time in life, even if we don't have too much of it. It is our resource, and we tend to apply it first to any problem.

Parents often believe that some of their financial resources will buy a nice safety net for their twenty-somethings, who haven't found their path of life yet. *Maybe we can support him for just a few more years,* they think. *Just long enough for him to figure out what he wants to do with his life.*

This can be a dangerous course, once it gets started, because no amount of money can buy the hard lesson of self-sufficiency; it's like sending your child to an ice-cream parlor in hopes that he'll lose weight. "I've seen parents willing to destroy themselves financially," says financial planner Bill Mahoney of Oxford, Massachusetts. "They're giving their college graduates $20,000, $30,000, even $40,000—money they should be plowing into retirement."[2]

> No amount of money can buy the hard lesson of self-sufficiency.

Our children become dependent on our handouts, and they will push the pipeline to its full capacity. Again, there isn't necessarily anything devious about this; our children believe they need the money and that their parents should give it to them. This is just part of immaturity.

But by this time of life, our young adult children can be fairly sophisticated in their thinking. They know us well, and they know how to get what they want. Our children can be very persuasive as they sit down with Dad in the study and talk about career plans that sound wonderful to us, then ask for the cash it will take to get going. And, of course, there are times when we can and should help them. For example, imagine that your son wants to get some extra education. He wants to go for a business degree at the local college, then get into the sales world. It's a worthy goal, but should you pull out the checkbook and guarantee his full tuition, textbooks, etc.?

Perhaps the right thing to do in this case is to say, "Son, I'm excited about your plans, I endorse them wholeheartedly, and I'm willing to pay for one semester. We'll watch eagerly to see how you do. Do you think you can get all A's? If so, I'll pay for another semester. I also expect you to get a part-time job at the mall so you can personally pay for textbooks and other incidentals."

This is a wise strategy because it teaches responsibility gradually. We give our child an attainable goal that will require effort and concentration. We move along with this course of training at his speed as he learns the lessons and grows in character. In the case of adolescents, we move from limited freedom to much more freedom as they prove they are worthy of it.

The hard decision comes when your child doesn't come through. Let's say he makes all A's but one B. He convincingly demonstrates to you that this particular professor never gives A's; your son worked hard, carried out all his assignments in good faith, but could not realistically earn an A. In that case, of course, you would be flexible and assume your son had really done all you asked.

But what about the gray areas? What if he got a B and a C? Then you might have to show tough love and say, "I'm sorry, son, but we talked about the requirements. I was hoping you would do better. I'm afraid you'll have to find another plan to come up with funds if you want to stay in school."

Yes, it's a difficult demand for permissive parents today. But it's the right approach if you want them to learn. If you handle them lovingly, wisely, and firmly—all the while making it very clear that the love is unconditional even though the funding is not—then I believe you won't have to worry, because (in terms of our case above) they will buckle down and bring home that all-A report card.

On the other hand, if you don't think your child has learned discipline and responsibility, watch out. He may try various strategies to manipulate the response he desires. He could make it clear that his anger is very destructive, because he knows that will upset his parents, and maybe they'll give him what he wants to avoid that outcome. He will use lifestyle issues as a wedge, making you believe that he will go to church regularly, avoid tattoos and alternative fashions, and follow the straight and narrow as long as you keep the funds flowing. To the extent that you fear being embarrassed by your children's public behavior, that approach could be powerful.

Here is another one, a young adult version of a strategy that even little children know. Your child might play one parent against the other. Most commonly, Dad holds firm and says, "I'm sorry, son. I can't help you this time." So the son goes to Mom. He presents a very brokenhearted countenance and tells her how the conversation went—how cruel and unyielding Dad was and how it hurts him to feel that his parents don't love him after all and don't care about his future. Mom, of course, is astonished and horrified. She has a few funds of her own she has saved up, perhaps for some bedroom furniture. "I'm going to help you," she says, "but this will be our little secret. Not a word of this to your father."

Mom doesn't know, and probably her son doesn't know either, that manipulation has occurred. Neither do any of them know what damage this is doing to the emotional journey of a young adult who is not learning to stand on his own. When the financial pipeline finally runs dry because Mom and Dad are broke, or when the parents finally become embittered at how their child has used them, or inevitably when Mom and Dad are gone, their son will still not know how to take care of himself. The best-case scenario is for him to learn it sooner rather than later, and to learn it through your loving guidance rather than through the hard knocks of being alone in the world.

> Parents need to keep a solid front through the entire process of raising children.

Parents, of course, need to keep a solid front through the *entire* process of raising children. They must agree on their policy, be consistent about it, and support each other completely. If not, they can expect that sooner or later, their children will exploit the differences between them.

PLEASANT BUT FIRM

How do you handle these potentially explosive situations that revolve around money—or any other issue, for that matter? You do so by being pleasant but firm. I can't repeat that phrase too much, because it's the key to keeping the channels of true training open between you and your child.

When it becomes apparent that your child is going to ask you for money or some other considerable resource, realize immediately that this is a key moment in your journey as a parent and your child's journey to becoming an emotionally mature adult. Do all you can to keep the conversation on a rational, loving basis. Use many of the strategies we discussed in the second chapter: keep eye contact, watch the tone of your voice, and use physical touch if you can. Be very gentle, pleasant, "quick to listen, slow to speak and slow to become angry, for man's anger does not bring about the righteous life that God desires" (James 1:19–20).

Pleasant is the tone, firm is the policy. If you have to decline the request you are given, explain your reasons for doing so lovingly but not defensively. Show that the right thing isn't always the easiest thing to do. If your child expresses anger, this is another time to remember the basics. Go ahead and let the anger be expressed verbally, because you don't want it to take root and express itself irrationally as stealth anger. But let's assume your son leaves in a huff, slamming the door behind him and promising you won't see him again. At the moment it may seem like an irreparable breach, but as a parent you must have better faith in the love

> Do all you can to keep the conversation on a rational, loving basis.

between you. You can't give in to what is just another form of emotional manipulation. Is it worth compromising his training down the road just to avoid the unpleasantness of being firm right now?

In the long run, children always respect the difficult lessons they have been taught. They will be appreciative that you helped them learn a principle of life that simply could not be learned any other way but the hard way. Just be certain that you don't allow the impasse to become an angry confrontation that closes off communication between you. You prevent this through your own self-control, through the power of the love that you express to your child, and by the pleasant but firm and consistent response with which you continue to guide your twenty-something through a rocky time in life.

WHAT ABOUT THEIR OWN MONEY?

Sometimes your child does have his own resources, but he still faces great challenges. He must still learn the difficult lessons of managing money. In the case of each of us, a great deal of immaturity is expressed in the way we handle money while we are growing up. Let's think of an example.

Peter is living at home while he pays off his college loan. He's making great progress in doing so, because his cost of living is practically nonexistent while he stays in his old bedroom. All week he works in an entry-level position at a local business, and it feels like drudgery to him. At the end of the week, he thinks about what a good job he has done in persevering. He thinks about how little money he would have saved if he had been out on his own, trying to keep an apartment and buy groceries. And by golly, he feels that he owes himself a reward. So he goes out and spends $1,500 on a new state-of-the-art stereo system with surround sound.

> In the long run, children always respect the difficult lessons they have been taught.

This is similar to the dieter who rewards himself with a big splurge at his favorite restaurant. It's easy to rationalize, but it's a backward step in reaching the goal we've set, and it opens the door to falling into some bad habits. It's disappointing to discover how often twenty-somethings move home to save money, then feel so liberated from the financial burden that they spend even *more* money. Part of the lure of spending, of course, is the fact they are frustrated. They don't really want to be living at home or working at the bottom level of their business field. They don't want to feel poor. So they spend as a way of experiencing a financial power they don't have.

There are many monetary traps for twenty-somethings today, because they represent the most desirable marketing target for advertisers. They can easily be seduced by the sports car whose payments seem affordable at first glance, or by the Colorado ski trip that they tell themselves is "worthwhile for networking with other career people."

Credit cards represent another trap. Many young people go out and get a new one every time they want to make a significant purchase. Then the debt accumulates on each card, with the interest demanded climbing as high as 30 percent or more. By the age of thirty, many naive young people have dug holes that will take a lifetime to climb out of. They mean well, and they really believe they can handle the debt, but in the end it is the debt that handles them.

> It's disappointing to discover how often twenty-somethings move home to save money, then feel so liberated from the financial burden that they spend even *more* money.

You can gently help your adult child learn to work with financial goals that will give him a sense of proud autonomy as his resources slowly grow and his debts slowly dwindle. The first step, of course, is to help him understand just how real the dangers are and just how merciless our world is toward those who can't pay their bills. Bankruptcy, for instance, has lifelong repercussions.

What about your own financial history? Can you use your own past mistakes and debt to help make a point that can help your child?

You might take him with you to visit a financial consultant who can explain, for example, the devious strategies of the credit card companies and show how quickly the high interest penalties can mount to a level that is completely unmanageable and life-disrupting (often marriage-disrupting). The adviser can also demonstrate just how wise and powerful a conservative savings plan can be.

> By the age of thirty, many naive young people have dug holes that will take a lifetime to climb out of.

GOALS AND GROWTH

Talk with your adult child about his financial goals. What would he really like to see happen in his life? Most young adults, of course, would like financial independence. They would like to have investments and savings that are growing, and they would like to be able to contribute to causes that matter to them. Naturally, they see themselves living in large homes some day and being able to give their own children what they need and want.

The next question is, "When would you like to reach that goal?" Most young adults will tell you they want to enjoy at least some success while they are still young. Therefore, they will need a plan to get to the goals, and of course they will reach the goal sooner if they put the plan into action sooner. All of this seems painfully obvious, but there are many times when twenty-somethings have not thought this far. They can have fantastically simplistic ideas about money and the attaining of wealth. Help your child understand the basics of reaching his financial goals:

• First, he will need to eliminate debt, and this must be done gradually over a reasonable period of time. Patience can be a hard lesson to learn. There is nearly always going to be debt, so we must learn to judge what debt is wise and what is unwise. Education and real estate are investments, so they are good and often necessary debts. A new car is not an investment because it devalues immediately.

• Second, he must begin to save money. This will require having a firm grip on what his income is and what his expenditures are, and seeing that the latter is less than the former. Help your child learn to create a working budget. If you want to give him a gift, give him a computer program such as Quicken or Microsoft Money to help him manage his budget. He will enjoy experiencing the process by which extra income becomes savings that accumulates interest. And, of course, we help our children see that get-rich-quick schemes almost always fail; there is no substitute for time plus consistency. "Dishonest money dwindles away, but he who gathers money little by little makes it grow" (Prov. 13:11).

• Third, he will need to learn restraint in spending. Everyone has an impulse to spend that tax refund on something pleasurable—a new television or laptop computer, perhaps— instead of the mundane but rewarding path of depositing the check into savings. Deferred gratification requires maturity, and it is the only way we can see our wealth grow.

• Fourth, help him understand the joy of giving. This is a true discipline when we are financially limited ourselves. Giving to church or to charity, however, is part of the growth of our character. It helps us focus outside ourselves, to the needs of others. Model this kind of generosity, and help your young adult child discover that even now, he can set aside a small amount for giving.

DO YOUR HOMEWORK

The financial world around us is complex, and most young adults are simply ignorant about it. When he was training his disciples, Jesus said, "I am sending you out like sheep among wolves. Therefore be as shrewd as snakes and as innocent as doves" (Matt. 10:16). Believe me, the financial world is a wolf-ridden one. Yet there are many wise strategies that can be adopted if we simply do our homework and help our children do so. You can show your adult child what a great difference it makes to simply have the facts about the help that is available.

For example, young adults today are very high on volunteer work. They're setting a terrific example for us in short-term missions projects, crisis relief, and other worthy goals. Did you know that the United States government will take care of outstanding educational loans in many cases where young people volunteer? Americorps offers a $4,725 credit toward loans and a $7,400 stipend for one year of service. The Peace Corps offers great financial assistance and deferment on loans in exchange for service (which can be a rewarding process in maturity in itself, of course). The National Guard and the Army Reserves offer up to $10,000 toward school loans.[3]

There are many more opportunities for young adults who can use their youth, their energy, and their ideals not only to help them reduce their debt, but to see the world and to grow in the strength of their character. As a matter of fact, I strongly recommend military service, Peace Corps, and missions work as worthwhile endeavors for your children, if they have thought and prayed about them and feel called in those directions.

They have an opportunity to learn a great deal about the world and themselves, and it might be harder to have that energy or freedom once they are married and settled down. Particularly in military service, they learn discipline that makes a dramatic difference

> We all need to know how to manage our money in a dangerous world filled with wolves who prey among the sheep.

in the rest of their lives. I have seen many cases of young people who have struggled to become emotionally mature and who seemed on the verge of creating terrible problems for themselves and their families, only to receive just what they needed from a short stint in the military.

Therefore, as you look at where your adult child is in the process of his life, take careful notice of how he handles the money he earns and the money you give him. If he is reckless in handling or naive about resources, it's a true danger sign. His inability to understand the value of money could even be something you take lightly now—an endearing eccentricity, it could seem—but that eccentricity could be the harbinger of heartbreak to come sometime in the future. We all need to know how to manage our money in a dangerous world filled with wolves who prey among the sheep, and where there are Internet scams, identity theft maneuvers, investment rackets, and other quickly evolving ways to separate you and your family from your hard-earned money.

On the other hand, if your child can wisely handle his money, that's a sign too. It demonstrates that he thinks not just about today but about tomorrow; it shows that he has a certain amount of personal discipline and restraint. And you can be certain that if he has these qualities, he has learned them from caring parents, and these virtues become ingrained habits that will see him toward a future of success and positive accomplishment. On a landscape of wreckage filled with the lives of other young men and women who failed to handle their finances and therefore their lives, your son or daughter could be a beacon of hope, someone who survived and thrived, and will help make a difference in the lives of many other people.

That's why you should explore the subject of money together right now, even if it's a difficult area for your family to discuss; even if your child considers it "his own business"; even if it could provoke an argument. We are what we spend, what we owe, and what we give—and your child is formulating his identity right now.

eight

JOB ONE: ONE JOB

The business world is puzzled. It doesn't know exactly what to make of this twenty-something generation.

Every new group of young adults, of course, constitutes the roster of the rising workforce. The best and the brightest men and women, often fresh out of college, are recruited into the corporations and sales organizations of America.

But in recent months, as supervisors compare notes, they find themselves scratching their heads about the problems of managing their newest hires. According to Claire Raines, an organizational consultant in Denver and co-author of *Twentysomething: Managing and Motivating Today's New Work Force*, there are increasing complaints about hiring new employees who never show up to work—or those who come in for months, shuttle through the company's expensive training process, then change their minds and quit.

Raines makes the point that for every employee who doesn't

work out, the rising cost of recruiting, hiring, and training has been wasted. Therefore, bosses are becoming less tolerant and more wary of anyone they bring into the organization.[1]

The problem is that the twenty-somethings are watching these companies with the same wariness. As a generation, they make up a relatively small segment of the workforce, yet a huge percentage of certain entry-level positions.

Therefore, the jobs and the young adults need each other—but they're not hitting it off too well. As we'll see, there is evidence that the young adults who *do* work are trying on and discarding jobs like a fickle woman shopping for a dress. They don't seem to be proactive about their intentions; they haven't decided what they want to be when they grow up.

> The jobs and the young adults need each other—but they're not hitting it off too well.

Instead, they are sampling wildly different options until they happen to run into one (if ever) that fits. Your child may announce he is going into the ministry, spend a few months in seminary, then try selling insurance for a year or two.

Raines says these younger employees "want balance and flexibility. They also want to do meaningful work, continue to learn and grow, and be able to make a contribution. That means taking your employees seriously and listening to their ideas."[2] Much is therefore written about how to relate to and communicate with these twenty-somethings, and Raines offers a detailed list of all the changes that an employer must make in order to be tolerated by the young workforce. The question is whether the employers are willing and able to make those changes to accommodate entry-level workers.

Here is yet another reason twenty-somethings are delaying

their lives, stalling at the entrance to their career paths, and moving back home to sort it all out. They are very uneasy about this whole business world that suddenly looms before them. After all, this is the rest of their lives they're talking about. They want their forty hours per week to *count* for something rather than merely punching the clock, participating in the group policy, going home to sleep, and getting up for another workday.

Dallas-based consultant Bradley Richardson, author of *JobSmarts for TwentySomethings*, says, "We've seen what has happened to our parents. We watched them dedicate their lives to corporations and then be blindsided by downsizing."[3]

It's a fair point. A generation of fathers worked loyally for their respective companies. They toiled for years to work their way slowly up the corporate ladder until they became a little too expensive to their organizations in salary and benefits—then they were unceremoniously cut loose. Business in America has changed; some would say our corporate world has lost its soul. After twenty years of mega-mergers and buyouts, there aren't really so many medium or small businesses left. Each industry seems to have its faceless multinational corporations who struggle for their billion-dollar shares of the pie. It's no wonder that many of us—not just twenty-somethings—have become deeply cynical about the business climate of this new world. Young adults care about issues such as protecting the environment, and they look at big business as the enemy rather than the place they plan to spend the rest of their lives.

> Business in America has changed; some would say our corporate world has lost its soul.

Just a few years ago, there were jobs opening everywhere for techno-savvy twenty-somethings. The dot-com revolution was bursting forward at full steam; here at last was a field where the younger you were, the better you were positioned to take advantage of the millions of dollars being thrown at Web ventures. Twenty-somethings were raised with the computer mouse in their hands. They were technologically fearless, and there were millions of dollars to be made when the new Internet appeared to be the most wide-open frontier since Westward expansion. If Andrew Greeley were still around, he might have said, "Go Web, young man!" But as we know, the exuberance faded in one great crash. Many young adults continue to work in IT or Net-driven jobs, but many of those businesses now look just as coldly corporate as a job in the mail room of U.S. Steel.

Twenty-somethings also study the corporate landscape and discern that the best jobs are already occupied by the baby boomers who make up their parents' generation. Finally they sigh with exasperation and say, "I'm not exactly certain whether I want to enter that arena or not. May I be a teenager for a little longer?"

It's not difficult to understand their disillusionment.

ALTERNATIVES TO MCJOBS

Merriam-Webster's Dictionary added a new word in 2003: *McJob*. It's a slang term referring to a low-paying, low-prestige, low-satisfaction position that offers few advancement opportunities and requires no real talent. Such work is seen as demeaning and depersonalizing. The source of the word, of course, is the McDonald's restaurant chain, where there is seemingly always room for another burger-flipper or drive-thru attendant.

This highly educated, highly talented, creative, and energetic generation is often unwilling to pay its initial dues by serving fast food or holding a shoehorn at the mall. Its young men and young women are deeply concerned that even if there is a prestigious job for them out there somewhere, it won't be satisfying and meaningful to them.

Meaningful is a very important distinction. At one time, people thought of work as something that paid the bills. That paradigm has certainly been replaced by the idea that we should all be pursuing our personal dreams rather than the best route to a good paycheck. The personal dream could be one's own restaurant venture, a career in music, the writing of the great American novel, or a shot at directing films in Hollywood. Today's best-selling books are self-help titles (of which you are holding an example) that often urge the reader to "go for it," to seize the day, and to let no one say you can't find the end of your personal rainbow. Even television plays on this idea. At this writing, the top-rated television show is *American Idol*, in which absolutely ordinary people audition for their chance to win a million-dollar recording deal. The greatest segment of viewers is the younger demographic, and many of them are buying into the idea that they can have it all and have it now.

We have a generation with stars in its eyes—and of course that's not completely a bad thing. We will always need dreamers, creative people, and entrepreneurs. On the other hand, if everyone is a recording star or a restaurant owner, who will work at the paper mill? Who will assemble automobiles in Detroit? Who will be our accountants and plumbers and roofing contractors? Who will keep America running in the countless mundane but essential tasks on which our daily lives depend?

As I talk to young adults today, I'm actually surprised to discover that they don't think much about the "career track." During the past year I had an injury that required intensive physical therapy. I hired a fitness organization that assigned young, qualified therapists to help me exercise and recuperate. I found that they were a delight not only in work but in conversation, and we got along wonderfully. These young men and ladies were highly efficient and passionate about their work, and also willing to discuss any subject, including spiritual ones (I believe twenty-somethings are far more comfortable talking about religion than past generations). They had a great sense of humor that lifted my heart during a difficult time.

However, what I also found was that these young people thought about everything but the future. We might normally expect that young adults fresh from college would be preoccupied with the whole idea of finding a career. That's just not who this generation is.

> As I talk to young adults today, I'm actually surprised to discover that they don't think much about the "career track."

While they take material things for granted—computers, cars, MP3 players—there are other ways in which they are far less materialistic, at least for now. They are *passion pursuers*. What's the best alternative to a McJob? It's one that has personal significance. My therapists happened to be twenty-somethings who were consumed by the idea of personal fitness—natural evangelists for their company who believed that everyone should be committed to their particular approach to health and wellness.

Many young adults are going into missions and social work too. The Peace Corps announced that it has accepted more new volunteers than at any time in thirty years—up 20 percent over the year 2000;[4] applications to Teach for America, which recruits graduates for underserved urban and rural areas, tripled in that same time span.[5] While charitable giving has decreased in recent years, volunteerism has gone up. While young people have very negative views of the political process, they are very optimistic about personal hands-on involvement. As a matter of fact, not only do they find meaning in giving their time and sweat to worthy pursuits, but they use it as a social vehicle for meeting friends and having fun.

Obviously there are many positive factors to this development. There are also some areas where we need to teach twenty-somethings to think with a little more focus and a bit more down-the-road perspective. My observation is that many of them drift into these exciting, meaning-oriented jobs and find wonderful fulfillment for several years—only to discover, a few years later, that they've hit the ceiling in terms of earnings just as they've become ready to own a home, have a family, and start a fund for educating their children. Some of them have sacrificed their most energetic years to start-up industries, recreational fads, or other bubbles that eventually burst. Sometimes it's a steady job that will simply never allow for the kind of career that might support a family.

Steve Rothberg, founder and president of College Recruiter.com, believes there are actually two of these seasons of life where young people tend to reverse their directions in terms of career interest. He writes that a twenty-five-year-old finds being an accountant makes him miserable. He panics about the idea of doing it for forty years, and therefore his highest priority is to feel better about his work. But at thirty-five he reacts in the other direction—now his greatest priority is his mortgage, his children, and his other obligations.[6] The trouble is that the older we become, the more difficult it is to backpedal.

THINKING ABOUT THE FUTURE

We need to help our adult children learn to think logically and objectively about the world of work. It's likely to be a thorny subject, of course. None of us particularly like to be told what we should be doing with our lives. We all think of the nagging mom who wants her son to be a doctor or a lawyer, while the young man has no sense of calling to either of those fields.

Just the same, there are ways you can promote an ongoing conversation that avoids being authoritarian and overbearing. Whether or not your twenty-something lives at home, would she be open to having a regular session for the purpose of chatting about future prospects over a good dinner? You could do this at your favorite Mexican restaurant or over a special menu at home, and you could create an anxiety-free, positive atmosphere of discussing and even dreaming about your adult child's potential and developing options. You'll find that your adult child isn't opposed to talking about work; she simply wants to talk about it on her own terms, in a nonpressured way.

> The trouble is that the older we become, the more difficult it is to backpedal.

As you converse, be sure to ask open-ended questions: How do you feel about your friend's new job over at the bank? What are the pros and cons of your brother's position in the insurance industry, from your point of view? What do you think it would feel like to be a salesperson and work for incentive pay? How much competition is there in this event-planner field that appeals to you so much? Who would be a good resource person for getting further information about it?

The ideal would be for your child to see you as a helpful

resource person rather than an ominous threat who couldn't possibly understand her goals and desires. You can't make big decisions for your children, and the more you push, the more unattractive you will make the decision you believe to be the best. The good teacher always lets the pupil come up with the answer, while guiding her right up to the place where she can find and consider that answer herself.

Even in that highly desired moment when your child actually says, "What do you think, Mom (or Dad)?" you should work toward helping her make the right decision herself. You could say, "I would imagine there are some real benefits and a few drawbacks to that job, as there are with any job. Why not make yourself a list of both? Draw a line down the center of the page, then list all the good things on one side and all the bad things on the other. Then we'll talk."

If your child makes such a list, you have the opportunity to go over it with her. "How much weight would you give this benefit," you might say, pointing to a particular line on the list, "compared to the others?" (As in the game show *Jeopardy*, everything should be phrased in the form of a question!) You might be able to guide your child to the realization that some benefits (such as "This job is fun!") could actually change over a couple of years, and others could seem more significant ("This job provides no insurance benefits or pension plans"). The point could

> The ideal would be for your child to see you as a helpful resource person rather than an ominous threat who couldn't possibly understand her goals and desires.

be gently made that in time, our perspectives and our values change. Such items as health insurance mean less to a twenty-five-year-old than to a forty-five-year-old. And what seems "fun" with a "!" right now is highly subjective. Will it seem fun five years from now? Even two years from now?

These thoughts, delivered as a sermon, will fall on deaf ears; offered as questions for contemplation, they could change a life.

THINKING ABOUT THE MEANING OF WORK

Career discussions also provide an exceptional opportunity for helping our children think about what is meaningful in life. You certainly have a practical point that a job needs to furnish the basic monetary resources that we need during the rest of life's journey. Your child has a point too: work should mean something. None of us want to feel that we are toiling in a generic corporation as a faceless employee doing mindless work for obscure purposes, no matter how well it pays or how much dental insurance is included in the group policy. We were made to work, and we want to find significance in our work.

But you can help your child see that there is meaning in all kinds of work, not just the dramatic opportunities with the Peace Corps (as wonderful as their service is) or serving as a river-rafting guide. From the beginning of the book of Genesis, the Bible teaches that we were made to find joy in many varieties of labor. Some people have advanced the misperception that work is a "curse" given to punish humanity for disobedience in the Garden of Eden. That is not the teaching of those chapters. Work is a gift, not a curse; God gave Adam and Eve the fulfilling assignment of tending the earth, caring for the animals, and starting families to populate the world.

> We were made to work, and we want to find significance in our work.

As a result, we find a great sense of accomplishment when we work. Think about a time when your family has labored together. It might have been raking, mowing, and doing other yard work. It might have been when you served elbow-to-elbow at a downtown soup kitchen. You can make the point to your child that when we perform work of any kind, it's not just what the work is that brings us joy—it's the work *itself*. We lose ourselves in performing a task well, and all the more so when we work together.

That could be a meaningful point for a young adult in your home. Twenty-somethings are usually at the peak of their personal health, ability, and capability. When they enter a negative cycle of drifting and waiting rather than working, they can become depressed. They need to be doing something productive that makes them feel good about the day and their own personal usefulness. Many of us become out of sorts when we don't have some task to perform, something to give us a sense of purpose. If you have a twenty-something at home who isn't employed and seems moody, you can help her by getting her off the sofa and into some kind of task that she might find absorbing. Dr. Mel Levine, author of *Ready or Not, Here Life Comes*, recommends that parents teach their children *how to work*. If your child is living at home, assign responsibilities and see that they're carried out. Show her how to manage her time and set priorities.[7]

It doesn't have to be a long-term job, just some assignment that could challenge her and make her feel useful, showing her the value of work and accomplishment and the satisfaction that comes from a job well done.

> If you have a twenty-something at home who isn't employed and seems moody, you can help her by getting her off the sofa and into some kind of task that she might find absorbing.

Oscar Hammerstein, who wrote the words to musicals such as *Show Boat*, *The Sound of Music*, and *Oklahoma*, once noted that the artists who sculpted the Statue of Liberty (which was presented originally as a gift to our nation from the French) took great pains to produce the individual hairs atop Liberty's head. As far as the sculptors knew, no one would ever see their work because it would be set high in the sky, far above the crowds who stood below. But that made no difference to the workers. God could see their handiwork! The point, of course, is that any work of excellence has a way of coming to light eventually. Sure enough, after the artists were finished with Lady Liberty, airplanes began to soar through the skies above New York City. It became possible to see the fine detail of the work after all.

> Any work of excellence has a way of coming to light eventually.

Work is significant and meaningful because we have put a little of ourselves into it. Many twenty-somethings haven't really ever had to work at anything harder than studying for an exam. They have the opportunity to discover the maturity and positive self-concept that come from doing a job and doing it well. They may not be able to start at the top. They may not be able to find a job that would make an exciting Hollywood movie. But they have the opportunity to earn their own way, which is pleasing in itself; and they have the joy of the job well done.

Imagine being a slave, who has no choice at all about what work to do. Here is the advice the apostle Paul gave to those in that lowly position:

Obey your earthly masters with respect and fear, and with sincerity of heart, just as you would obey Christ. Obey them not only to win their favor when their eye is on you, but like slaves of Christ, doing the will of God from your heart. Serve wholeheartedly, as if you were serving the Lord, not men, because you know that the Lord will reward everyone for whatever good he does. (Eph. 6:5–8)

The sculptors of the Statue of Liberty didn't care whose eye was on their work. They took pride in their accomplishment, and hopefully they realized that the eye of God is always on our work. We're not all about our work as much as the work is all about us. It should please us internally, because God gave us the ability to do it, and because he is the one who placed this opportunity before us. With that outlook, we are likely to find any job to be a labor of love.

Can you help your adult child think about the joy and meaning of work in general? Can you help her see that it's up to *her*, not the job, to provide the pleasure and fulfillment she seeks?

Having said that, it's also true that we want our children not to simply grab the first opportunity that comes along but to intentionally find the job that fits them best. Let's talk about how to do that.

MATCHING WORK TO WORKER

Allow me to make this point up front and as clearly as possible: young adults need to be trained in fields that bring a good return. Many of our children are graduating with degrees in, say, literature or music, and I'm certain there are good reasons for focusing on those subjects in education (particularly if one intends to teach). A good liberal arts education has many benefits. But a twenty-five-year-old who suddenly needs to support herself is going to have trouble doing so if she has devoted her education to becoming an expert in English poetry of the nineteenth century. Think about the tens of thousands of dollars we pay for a college education today and the years that will be spent repaying college loans. Do we and our children really want to invest that money and educational time in something we're not certain will be able to support one person, let alone a family? Isn't it still possible to study the liberal arts subjects out of personal interest, while devoting the major course of study to learning an occupation that will offer financial support and pave the way toward a home for your child and a good life for your grandchildren?

In a recent survey by *Time* magazine, it was discovered that the twenty-something generation had spent considerable amounts of money on education yet didn't consider itself ready for careers. Nearly one in five said that school did not prepare them to be successful in their work life. Nearly half the respondents had worked in two or three different workplaces during the past three years (one in twenty had worked in six or more!).[8] The conventional wisdom is that these younger adults will move laterally from job to job, almost at random, until they find the one that fits.

> If you still have children in college, encourage them to focus on a practical field that interests them.

Is all that job-hopping truly necessary? Isn't it possible to lay out a well-considered strategy as we reach adulthood and show some perseverance in sticking to a field? If you still have children in college, encourage them to focus on a practical field that interests them. There are countless options for jobs that are always needed in society that offer a good living and the possibility of advancement. Near the end of this chapter you'll find resources to help you find the growth industries that are the best bet for young people just entering the business world. If your child absolutely can't stand the idea of becoming an accountant or a stockbroker, naturally she shouldn't enter either field. But she should find a field she *can* enjoy that happens to provide the possibility of earning a solid living.

So how does she decide what that job should be? We're very fortunate in that regard. During the last few years, many good, in-depth personality evaluations have been developed that help us understand how we think, what we do well, and where we would fit. One of the classics is the Minnesota Multiphasic Personality Inventory (MMPI). This assessment is based on organizing the various types of personalities and showing how the test subject fits into the set categories. In recent years, the Myers-Briggs inventory, with its sixteen common types, has been even more popular. It places the test subject in ranges between series of dichotomies: extroversion versus introversion; sensing versus intuition; thinking versus feeling; and judging versus perceiving. There are many other helpful tests as well.

> Vocationally oriented personality testing can be very helpful to your young adult child in helping her begin to think about her place in the world of work.

Naturally, there are questions about the limitations of testing. For one thing, testing doesn't necessarily measure objective reality as much as it shows how we perceive ourselves—because, of course, we are the ones who make the evaluations that lead to the answers on those inventories. All the same, vocationally oriented personality testing can be very helpful to your young adult child in helping her begin to think about her place in the world of work. God has given her definite gifts, and those gifts were given for a reason. Our children need to understand that life is more than a random series of events where we hope to someday come across the right destiny. We are already equipped for that destiny, and we simply need to evaluate our tools and find out where they fit the best. A personality inventory might suggest that your child would be happiest working with numbers, doing some kind of people-driven work, or some field she hasn't even considered.

Having sized up the worker, it's time to size up the job market to make the best match. There are many ways of finding out the best available opportunities. The U.S. Department of Labor (http://www.dol.gov) offers an annually updated Occupational Outlook Handbook that gives the best information about what jobs are available: the training and education needed for them; the earnings; the expected job prospects; what workers do on the job; and what the working conditions are. Currently the Department of Labor advises that health services constitute the fastest-growing industry due to the fact that people are living longer. Technology and information services are ever-changing and always filled with opportunities, if your young adult child keeps up with the latest trends and has good training. The hospitality industry is also growing quickly. Within any of these particular fields (just a few of a great number of examples), there are many options for the kind of work that could be pursued. Health services, for example, represent everything from desk jobs to hands-on therapists, such as the ones who helped me, to research or many other options.

Your local bookstore offers a number of current guides to the best jobs. It pays to do the research. Also, don't forget to size up the particular community you live in, if this is the place your adult child will seek a career. What are the big companies in your area?

Who are some workers there who could tell you about the opportunities so that you could determine how well your child would fit?

Finally, career counseling can be very helpful. Again, this is a great option for the parent who wants to help the young adult child. Rather than give her a cash handout, pay for her appointment with a qualified job counselor who can not only give those helpful personality tests, but size up the untapped potential of a twenty-something and make an educated recommendation about her very best prospects. These counselors will also help with some of the common problems that plague young adults when it comes to fitting into the job field: motivation, procrastination, time management, and so on. I would recommend this route as a solid investment in the future of your child.

If you've done all these things—opened the doors of communication, guided your child toward focused thinking, helped her consider the meaning of work and the practicalities of what makes a good job, then finally helped her consider her own potentialities and what is available in the marketplace, you've done good work, my friend. You've laid a foundation for your child to make her very best effort to find her way in the career world, and the more preparation and research you have done, the better her chances will be of making a good match with the career you find together.

That doesn't mean she will immediately locate her dream job, of course. There is no guarantee that she won't do what so many young adult workers are doing today: "job surfing" until they find their comfort zone. The workplace is simply a more challenging environment than it has ever been. There will surely continue to be little permanence in the job world; little loyalty to the corporation from either the employee's or the employer's perspective. And businesses will come and go with frightening abruptness in this new cultural world around us. But somehow our children will do what every generation of workers has done. They will find their places, gradually make their own impact, and eventually they will mold the business world in their own image, just as their parents, the baby boomers, have done; just as the "Greatest Generation" before them did it; just as the forefathers of our country did at the end of the eighteenth century. They'll find their place.

And there's reason to be hopeful about that. Our twenty-something children are confused and struggling in many ways, but they have great hearts. They truly care about people, and they will refuse to let their work environments become centers of depersonalizing greed. They will bring into the boardroom what they are learning on missions trips to Haiti or Kenya, or through inner-city missions efforts and Habitat house-building projects. They just may find a way to help corporate America find its soul again.

> Our twenty-something children are confused and struggling in many ways, but they have great hearts.

I admit, it's hard to visualize all of that when your twenty-something is lying on the sofa listlessly watching television. She seems to be in no hurry to clean her room, much less change corporate America. She's taking an awful long time to get started in doing anything. But with your support and encouragement, once she does, she will achieve great things. We can trust God for that, and watch the results with pleasure as we grow older.

nine

DATING AND RELATING

Jeffrey, age twenty-eight, dreads going to family reunions.

While he was growing up, he knew he would hear it five or six times: "My, how you've grown! What grade are you in now?"

That line has given way to a new one. Now, as soon as they spot Jeffrey, every aunt, uncle, cousin, and grandparent is bound to say, "Tell the truth, Jeffrey, is there some special girl? When are you going to settle down and raise a family?"

Jeffrey never knows exactly how to answer that question. The truth is that he has asked it of himself often enough.

When his parents dropped him off at college at the beginning of his freshman year, he envisioned certain things for his life. He would finish school in four years (it eventually took five and a half); he would emerge with a career vision and a great job waiting for him (it didn't happen); and he would be engaged to marry his college sweetheart (that didn't happen either).

Whatever happened to college sweethearts? That's what Jeffrey's parents were. They met in school at a fraternity/sorority dance. What could be more old-fashioned than that? It was right out of an old movie. They were married at twenty-one, proud owners of a little ranch-style house at twenty-three, and parents at twenty-four. By the time they were twenty-eight, Jeffrey's age, they had two kids, two cars, two cats, and ten committee memberships at church. It wears out Jeffrey just to think about it!

His mom and dad don't get along perfectly all the time; at times they simply seem to coexist. But at least the folks seem to have their lives and their roles all figured out. Jeffrey has to admit that his own life seems to be stuck in neutral. At least he's moved out of the spare bedroom at home (Mom and Dad live in a much bigger house with a swimming pool now). Jeffrey works in technical support at a software company, which is at least acceptable as a job, for the time being. It requires him to talk to angry customers over the phone for eight hours every day. But at least he's in some kind of a steady position with a (barely) acceptable salary and decent benefits. Many of his friends haven't even gotten that far.

> Jeffrey is afraid to get married . . . yet he's afraid not to.

A few years ago, Jeffrey served as best man in the wedding of Jared, his former roommate. It was one of those ceremonies right out of a glossy bridal magazine. The whole shindig must have easily cost tens of thousands of dollars, especially considering the big reception with a band, champagne, and dancing. All the old gang were there. As Jared and his new Mrs. roared off to the airport in a limousine, on their way to a classic Hawaiian honeymoon, Jeffrey found himself very envious and more than a little bit lonely.

It wasn't the big ceremony or the fancy reception or even a trip to the islands that he coveted. Jeffrey wished he had a *soul mate* as Jared did. He wished he was totally in love, so much so that he could stake the rest of his life on it. Even at the young age of twenty-eight, Jeffrey has always had a deep-rooted fear that he would wind up alone, with all of his friends married or moved away. On Saturday nights he would sit by himself in front of a television in some cold apartment, watching rented movies and sending out for pizza. The thought was so depressing that Jeffrey decided then and there that he was going to find his soul mate, just as Jared had.

For about three years Jeffrey dated, but nothing serious developed. Then, late one night, there was a knock at the door. It was Jared. "Can I crash with you?" he asked.

Jared was trembling as he explained that his wife had found someone else and kicked him out. A terrible argument had ensued. Why should Jared leave? He was co-owner of the house they had recently bought. He was also the father of the child the couple had brought into the world together.

Jeffrey is a horrified observer as he watches the legal melodrama that has followed. A divorce cannot be granted to Jared and his wife because all the property and guardianship issues are tied up in court—they could remain so for *years*. The "soul mates" cannot agree on anything except the fact that both young adults are sinking deep into debt as they pay lawyers to protect their interests. You'd think they could call a cease-fire just to save thousands of dollars, but there seems to be no solution. Jeffrey sees what all of this unpleasantness has done to the demeanor of his formerly happy-go-lucky friend—and he wonders how it will affect the child.

And his relatives want to know when he plans to settle down?

What a question. Jeffrey is afraid to get married . . . yet he's afraid not to.

THE STATE OF THE UNIONS

The National Marriage Project, sponsored by Rutgers University, conducted a survey on young adults and the state of marriage in our country. Among their findings was this analysis:

> Young adults today are searching for a deep emotional and spiritual connection with one person for life. At the same time, the bases for marriage as a religious, economic or parental partnership are receding in importance for many men and women in their twenties. Taken together, the survey findings present a portrait of marriage as emotionally deep and socially shallow.

- An overwhelming majority (94 percent) of never-married singles agree that "when you marry you want your spouse to be your soul mate, first and foremost."

- Less than half (42 percent) of single young adults believe that it is important to find a spouse who shares their own religion.[1]

It's interesting, isn't it? In a landslide victory, the soul mate advocates win the election. They are looking for a separate human being to share a common soul, if we understand the term correctly. Where does that idea come from? The Bible, of course. In the creation story of Adam and Eve, the woman is created from bone of the man's bone and flesh of his flesh. In other words, they are of the same essence. The stated conclusion is: "For this reason a man will leave his father and mother and be united to his wife, and they will become one flesh" (Gen. 2:24).

Marriage, then, is a kind of restoration of what was originally intended: one complete human unit composed of male and female who have come together in a way that is much more than legal, much more than social—it is supernatural. The *soul*, after all, is not found in any anatomical references. It is a matter of faith; our understanding of the spirit that dwells within each of us.

A soul mate, then, is a faith designation, whether we recognize it as such or not. Those who yearn for a soul mate believe there is someone created just for them, someone who can commune with them in the deepest parts of their being in such a way that the two become one.

But even as nearly nineteen out of twenty people affirm their quest for that soul mate, how is it that only eight out of that same twenty (about 42 percent) "believe that it is important to find a spouse who shares their own religion"? What is wrong with this picture?

We are a religious people who have forgotten the religious basis of our need. Marital counselors, particularly church pastors, will tell you that is true of young couples of mixed-faith backgrounds, or no-faith backgrounds, all the time. They seem prepared to discuss nearly every issue, right down to what color the trim on the fine china should be. The exception is matters of faith; that one simply doesn't seem important to them, or it is an underlying tension that they imagine will sort itself out someday.

> Those who yearn for a soul mate believe there is someone created just for them, someone who can commune with them in the deepest parts of their being in such a way that the two become one.

It would be too easy to blame all this on the younger generation. Don't we as the church (and possibly as parents) deserve some of the blame? Twenty-somethings don't see the relevance of organized religion to such real-world matters as dating and marriage. Among those who have grown up in church, they haven't particularly observed that faith provides sanctuary from divorce—the marital breakup rate is at least as high as in the secular world.

Meanwhile, they keep hearing that should they take a partner to the altar, they have a 50 percent chance of divorce. Young adults like Jeffrey, yearning for that soul mate, finally take a step backward as fear wins out. They don't want marriages that end in strife, as so many of their parents have experienced. Even now, some of their friends are already experiencing rocky romances. What are they to do? What are we to tell them? And is it possible that God might still have something to offer when it comes to a soul searching for its mate?

> Twenty-somethings don't see the relevance of organized religion to such real-world matters as dating and marriage.

IT'S NOT ABOUT YOU

The first lesson we must teach our young adult children is that life is more than simply fulfilling personal desires, and it's even about more than simply making one other person happy. It's illuminating to look closely at the work done by the National Marriage Project cited earlier. The results of the researchers painted a picture of the young adult view of marriage that is "emotionally deep and socially shallow." What exactly does that mean?

The twenty-somethings resonated powerfully with the term

"soul mate." They seem to be looking for a profound, deeply fulfilling relationship with another person. And it almost seems as if any other consideration about the meaning of marriage is completely overshadowed by this need. Young men and women are looking for what Shel Silverstein's children's book called The Missing Piece.[2] It is the idea of the one person in the world who will interlock with you or me perfectly. The popular Tom Cruise film *Jerry Maguire* introduced the catchphrase "You complete me." It entered the popular lingo so quickly that we know it touched a nerve.

Twenty-somethings feel a yawning emptiness that cries out for a fulfilling relationship. They are *very* relational people who want to have many friends, but they also want to find the "significant other." On the one hand, they see what happens when marriages go wrong, as Jeffrey has seen with his friend Jared (and, to a much lesser extent, his parents). They still feel they can find that missing piece, but it's going to take quite a search, and they're going to have to be completely certain.

Jeffrey Arnett, the creator of the term "emerging adulthood," says that twenty-somethings are, if anything, too romantic. They will go through relationships like Goldilocks goes through porridge until she finds the bowl that is "just right." When they finally marry, they want perfection. Arnett says, "Everybody wants to find their soul mate now, whereas I think, for my parents' generation—I'm forty-seven—they looked at it much more practically. I think a lot of people are going to end up being disappointed with the person that's snoring next to them by the time they've been married for a few years and they realize it doesn't work that way."[3]

> Twenty-somethings feel a yawning emptiness that cries out for a fulfilling relationship.

What have they missed? What are the "practical" dimensions that Arnett's parents considered? It could be that previous generations were more simple and less dramatic in their demands for a loving mate with whom to build a family and a life. There was a lot less talk about "completing" each other half a century ago. Romantic love was surely part of the equation. But people realized (as we should always realize) that the early euphoria of infatuation cannot last; it gives way soon enough to hard work, done side by side, to earn the keep, to keep the house, and to raise the children. And there wasn't really the option of a decade-long quest to find the perfect soul mate. It was understood that marriage comes in the late teens or the early twenties. Children were due to arrive in relatively short order, and preferably a station-wagon-load of them.

> The early euphoria of infatuation cannot last; it gives way soon enough to hard work, done side by side, to earn the keep, to keep the house, and to raise the children.

When Dad has his hands full with work that brings home the necessities to feed a household, and Mom has her hands full with creating a loving home for those children, there isn't a lot of time left for hand-wringing over the little imperfections of the relationship. And it should also be added that husbands and wives often needed to work a bit harder on their relationship during those years; though there were fewer divorces, there was probably just as much unhappiness.

In the past, couples were surely not so romantic in the sentimental sense of that word. Marriage was a very serious commitment meant to last a lifetime, but its true foundation was the selfless work of building a family, not the self-driven pursuit of being enraptured by a soul mate.

What, then, do we want to teach our young adult children? We're not pushing them to hurry up and select a mate as they would select an apple from the tree. Their seriousness about emotionally deep relationships is a good thing. But we want them to see the big picture. We want them to understand that the romantic idea of a perfect match is unrealistic—any relationship takes hard work and plenty of grace and forgiveness. And we want to help them understand that marriage is about far more than the meeting of personal needs. It is about toiling together over the decades to build a future—for our homes, for our neighborhoods, for our world. The less we focus on ourselves and the more we focus on giving ourselves away, the more and the deeper we will find that we love each other.

There is also the parenting angle to consider. We talk to young married couples these days and find that many of them have waited until they were in their mid-thirties to marry. In this way, it's arguable that they've had the advantage of bringing more wisdom and emotional maturity to the marriage. On the other hand, by the time they have settled down together, it could be too late for children. Many childless couples are very happy, of course—they do have a freedom to take off, for example, on weekend trips or mission endeavors on a moment's notice.

But it's also undeniable that the raising of children is one of the deepest and most fulfilling pleasures life can offer. Children are a blessing from the Lord that is like no other gift he could offer us. With this in mind, we hear the young couples say, "Yes, indeed, we have a child! It's our little wirehaired terrier. She keeps us entertained all the time, and it's just like having a child around the house." We understand what is meant here, but we want to say, "Oh, but a pet dog is not like having a child at all! You can't imagine how amazing an experience it is to bring a tiny human being into the world. It's a blend of your combined genes as a couple but also a new and unique human being. You can't imagine what it's like to teach her to speak and to read, to see her grow into maturity."

Surely we can agree that marital love is about so much more than finding someone to make me feel good, and making her feel good too. It's not about me, really. It's about finding my humble but useful place in the future of this world. Because only through my children, and through my training of them, can the unique DNA fingerprint that is created by God, and that constitutes *me*, have an impact on the generations yet to come.

As for that elusive soul mate, yes, many married couples become just that. When we are willing to work at it, offer unconditional love and daily grace, we find that marriage at its best begins to look like the optimal friendship. It may not have the wild passion of early infatuation, but who would truly want to prolong that craziness anyway? It has something better: a deep commitment to go through life hand in hand, helping each other along, for better or for worse, in sickness and in health.

> Children are a blessing from the Lord that is like no other gift he could offer us.

It's also worth mentioning that the ultimate soul mate is available to us all. It's interesting to listen to Jesus talking to his disciples in the Upper Room the night before he is to be taken away from them and crucified. He says that as he leaves, the Holy Spirit will come in his place. That will allow Jesus to be "with" each of us in a new way:

> I will not leave you as orphans; I will come to you. Before long, the world will not see me anymore, but you will see me. Because I live, you also will live. On that day you will realize that I am in

my Father, and you are in me, and I am in you. Whoever has my commands and obeys them, he is the one who loves me. He who loves me will be loved by my Father, and I too will love him and show myself to him. (John 14:18–21)

Jesus says, "I am in my Father, and you are in me, and I am in you." This is indeed a profound passage, yet one that should have incredible relevance for twenty-somethings who feel a deep desire for perfect fellowship with a kindred soul. Jesus is the bridge between God and his lonely children. And when we love him and obey him through living, as Jesus describes here, we see him in a unique way. He lives through us, and we experience his joy.

In other words, we want our children to love and to serve God by living a good life of service to others. And the Spirit of God himself will take residence in our hearts so that we can never be truly lonely. I realize we've moved into faith territory here (in a chapter on marriage and relationships). But the wonderful offer that Jesus makes is one that has tremendous bearing, in so many ways, on the lives of these emerging young adults who are trying to make sense of life, of work, and of relationships.

Even with a healthy faith, our young adult children need to connect in a meaningful way with real flesh-and-blood people of their age. They yearn for human love and friendship in the form of a lifelong mate. In time, they will "audition" various love interests who could become that soul mate they're seeking. At some time or other, they'll bring a date home to meet their parents, and they'll want to know what Mom and Dad think. They'll be seeking our approval, but whether they realize it or not, they'll also be seeking our guidance. Over time, how often has this question been asked of parents: *How will I know when I meet the right one?*

Let's discuss some principles for guiding your adult child in the area of relationships.

HOW DO I KNOW?

A young man like Jeffrey has figured out an unsettling truth after witnessing Jared's experience. He perceives that it's possible to marry someone only to discover we didn't know them nearly as well as we thought. It happens again and again today, and unfortunately it happens quite frequently in Christian contexts too; there's no escaping the problems in our modern culture. A person puts up a good front, seems to have all the right values, and then the mask comes off when the honeymoon is over.

> The current culture has poisoned the environment for selfless, committed love between people.

The question, then, is how to help your child see past the mask. Your son or daughter wants to know if it's still possible to ensure a divorce-proof marriage at the commitment stage. I hate to sound pessimistic, but there is a reason so many younger people fail at marriage. The current culture has poisoned the environment for selfless, committed love between people. Anger has gone unmanaged in great numbers of people. In our model of stealth anger in the third chapter, we saw that it was possible for a person to seem quite healthy and normal for a period of time before the anger emerged destructively yet again. And we see this in marriages as well as everywhere else. Young men and women are bringing old, unmanaged anger issues into their marriages. Their spouses are paying the price for unresolved conflicts that may have happened years ago—and they are completely blindsided by this development.

Therefore, we need to train our children to be very perceptive and discerning about people. To quote again those words of Jesus, our children need to be "as shrewd as snakes and as innocent as doves" (Matt. 10:16). That means being gentle and loving without being naive and gullible. So I encourage them to watch for the hidden traces of true character. I advised my own children, for example, to observe how a boyfriend or girlfriend treats other people when they are not required to be nice. Let me explain what I mean.

Imagine you go to a restaurant with a business associate. The man is warm and cordial to you, as business requires him to be. But when the waitress brings one wrong item in his dinner order, he really reads her the riot act. Later, when someone cuts in front of him in traffic, he sits on the horn and curses. When you observe such an action, you have just learned something far more telling and more authentic about your friend than the possibly artificial deference he shows to you. I asked each of my kids to be observant in this way, and they found it to be a very helpful exercise in finding out who people really were.

A requirement to make a good evaluation, of course, is time. Now we could seem to be sending mixed messages to twenty-somethings in this regard—on the one hand, we're saying, "Hurry up and get on with your adult life!" On the other, we're saying, "Not so fast! Make sure you know your mate." The truth is that we often see young people delay their actual willingness to settle down—but then, deciding they're ready, they pursue the whirlwind courtship and marriage immediately after meeting someone on a two-week cruise or a ski

> We need to train our children to be very perceptive and discerning about people.

trip. Spontaneous, barely considered actions seem to be more and more common today.

The bottom line is that readiness for marriage and assurance about one particular partner are obviously two different issues. We emphasize again that young people can be very romantic; therefore they can push sound, rational thinking away in favor of Hollywood stereotypes such as "love at first sight." There is simply no substitute for taking the time to get to know someone; to see them in many different contexts and environments; to get some idea about what their family life has been like; and to discover the long-term pattern of their existing significant friendships. When it comes to finding the right person, time is truly on our side.

I also strongly recommend premarital counseling. However, let me warn you that many churches do a great disservice in this area. They offer a hurried counseling session or two that amount to a rubber-stamp approval of a relationship that really hasn't been closely examined. If, say, the young man or young lady has grown up in that church and has family there, the pastor may be in a difficult position. He has known the family for years, and he is reluctant to offend someone. He may also lack sound counseling credentials.

> You may have to look around to find qualified premarital counseling, particularly from the perspective of your faith. But it's worth doing.

You may have to look around to find qualified premarital counseling, particularly from the perspective of your faith. But it's worth doing. In accordance with such an evaluation, personality testing can be helpful. In the previous chapter we discussed some of these popular inventories that help us understand what kind of people we are and how we correspond to the other person.

And although we observe that Christian marriages, in general, are faring just as poorly as the rest, I believe faith backgrounds should be a good fit between a man and a woman who wish to marry. Surely this issue should come up between them long before they get to the stage of discussing the spending of their lives together; spirituality should be at the very basis of our self-understanding. How can we truly build toward marital intimacy without ever alluding to what we believe about God and how he relates to us in everyday life? I would encourage a believing couple to pray together and ask God from the beginning to cement their commitment together. In doing

> I would encourage a believing couple to pray together and ask God from the beginning to cement their commitment together. In doing so, the vows at the wedding will be more authentic and more binding than merely decorative words.

so, the vows at the wedding will be more authentic and more binding than merely decorative words. If we truly believe our Lord is real and powerful, how can we assume he is incapable or unwilling to help us work through marital problems, whatever they may be? I can't imagine going into marriage without an understanding that God is the third person in the union, and that we will turn to him humbly and sacrificially whenever we stumble.

I counsel young couples to really work at these understandings before they marry; one or two short sessions are inadequate. They do need to ask the big questions: How long before we start a family? How many children do we want? How will we raise them, and what are our feelings about the principles of parenting? Where do we want to live, and have we checked out the quality of schools in that area? Who is going to work, and what is his or her career vision?

How are we going to handle disagreements? How will we manage our anger? How will we manage our money? What about dealing with in-laws? What about church involvement? Time committed to hobbies or other pursuits? Which habits or personality traits are likely to be stumbling blocks in the long run, and what should we be doing about those issues now? What are our personal strengths and weaknesses?

Couples become so intent on picking out the china and basking in the glow of engagement that they tend to avoid the questions they find awkward and unpleasant. Such avoidance is a very dangerous way to proceed, because some of those issues could be time bombs. They are much easier to deal with now than later. And if there are just too many areas of basic incompatibility, isn't it better to find that out right now and avoid becoming another divorce statistic?

Time, wise judgment, observation, and prayer—your child will need all these things, and he'll need your help to apply them.

HELPING THEM WITH MARRIAGE

I hope I haven't made marriage sound like an obstacle course too difficult to complete. If you have raised your children well, help them but trust them; they want to do the right thing, and they simply need a little loving and gentle guidance. But of course, that guidance will no doubt continue long after the wedding bills have been paid (even as expensive as modern weddings can be!).

When your young adult child marries, another rite of passage has been reached. He has taken one more step away from the nest and toward the fruitful adult life that is your prayer for him. In taking note of that fact, of course, you realize that you will relate to him in a slightly different way now. This is the moment established at the dawn of time, recorded in the book of Genesis, when a "man will leave his father and mother and be united to his wife" (Gen. 2:24). In other words, he has established his own family unit now. He will always be your child, and you will always be his parents, yet things have changed a bit. Even though he is new at heading a household, he now has that responsibility. It's his show, though you will continue to be able to offer a certain amount of guidance under certain conditions. There is a subtlety in our parental adjustment to dealing with our children once they are married.

You will see him make mistakes, or at least do things differently from the way you did them. You'll be tempted to say something about it. You'll want to ask questions and give advice, but you'll need to show a loving and respectful restraint about these impulses. He respects you both as parents, and you also owe a certain measure of respect to him in his new role. We want our children to know, even as they prepare to marry, that we don't intend to interfere with their marriage in any way; we are simply here to help, as much or as little as they desire and require.

> It's very hard for parents to let go and let their children carry the burden of responsibility. If we don't let go, they'll never become mature, responsible adults themselves.

You will say, "Son, I once went over your school subjects with you. I asked about each subject, checked your progress, and guided you in the directions I thought you should go. I won't be doing that now that you're married. I will call to chat, and to exchange news, but I won't be trying to evaluate how you handle each little part of being a husband. If you ask for help, it will always be there for you. If you need someone to talk to, we're always here. But in no way will we violate the boundaries of your own home."

Your child will appreciate that, and he'll feel your respect as well as your love. But you'll find this new arrangement quite a challenge at times. It's very hard for parents to let go and let their children carry the burden of responsibility. If we don't let go, they'll never become mature, responsible adults themselves. And our presence on the sidelines of their marriage can cause an extra tension they don't need.

I want to add an extra caution about advice, particularly in the area of your grandchildren. Naturally your child will come to you and ask you a hard question at some time or other. "You've been a parent longer than me," he'll say. "What would you do?"

If it is a very difficult issue, I urge you not to answer too quickly or say too much. Say what you know for certain to be true, but don't rush ahead, trying to solve the whole problem. It's very easy to rush in where angels fear to tread. It is then that we can easily make a mistake and give bad advice, particularly when we're working from secondhand information. One of the smartest answers we can ever give is, "Let me think about that." Frankly it's a delay tactic for protecting yourself from saying the wrong thing. Time is your friend. You'll be able to discuss the problem with your spouse and perhaps a wise and mature friend, or maybe the problem will work itself out. You might even decide *not* to give any advice or make any endorsement of strategy to your children. Discretion is the better part of valor.

And when it comes to your child's marital problems, you can actually cause a great deal of damage by counseling your own children. We are far from biased in those situations. We are likely to be hearing one side of the story, and our emotions can overcome our wisdom. In such a situation, the very best option is to refer our children to a professional and objective counselor. At the very least, it's better to use the delay tactic than to blurt out emotional advice in the heat of the moment.

LIFESTYLE ISSUES

Many parents want to know how to handle disagreements about important issues of lifestyle and identity. The two most common are homosexuality and extramarital sexual activity, particularly cohabitation.

In our time, we've seen a radical change in the way society looks at the homosexual orientation. Over time, of course, this variation on the male/female establishment of sexuality has been opposed by virtually every world religion. In recent years we have come to a point where there is debate over same-sex unions being legally accepted as marriage. In Hollywood, the music world, and even in some political situations, our culture expects all people to look on the "gay" identity as completely normal and virtuous.

Your twenty-something child is far more likely to have and respect gay friends than someone from past generations. These young people are very comfortable with open, anything-goes sexuality because our culture has been deteriorating for their entire lifetime. But what if you have discovered that your child is homosexual himself and attracted to members of the same gender? For many parents, of course, it's a heartbreaking discovery. They love their child deeply, and therefore they want to be accepting and not condemning. Just the same, these parents most likely had dreams of grandchildren and a "traditional" family for

> Your twenty-something child is far more likely to have and respect gay friends than someone from past generations.

their child. There can be incredible tension and even division in families over this issue.

Let me recommend again what we have always urged in relation to family love: love *unconditionally*. We can do that without being in total agreement with every decision they make. We love those in our church who have different beliefs on certain issues, and certainly we will continue to love our children. Most parents are probably incapable of *not* loving them. The critical point is to reaffirm this with our children; they need to be able to clearly see and believe that even if we don't agree with or support certain decisions—whether it's a decision to pursue a certain career or affirm a certain sexual identity—we will never stop loving them. Make every possible effort to keep your communication and friendship with your child as strong as ever.

Your child, of course, will want your blessing. You have raised him in such a way that your endorsement of his decisions will make him feel better about them. You may have to lovingly disagree with him on those decisions. The biblical stance is that God loves every one of us, and all of us are sinners: men and women, church folks and the unchurched, heterosexuals and homosexuals. None of us are without the impurity of falling short of what God wants for us. So we deny Christian love to no one. In terms of a person's action, we take the stance that being homosexual in attraction is no sin at all, simply a temptation like any other. It is homosexual *activity* that Christians consider to be disobedience before God. Therefore, it is possible for a homosexual young person to live a chaste and obedient life, denying those impulses as we might deny

> What is important is to have a redemptive approach to any situation or challenge in life.

the impulse to overeat or to lose our temper or give in to the abuse of alcohol.

That stance won't be a comfortable one. Your child may argue that homosexual activity is no different from heterosexual activity, because that is the argument our culture has made, and it has been repeated until it seems that nearly everyone believes it. Each of us must make a decision whether to adhere to the stance of Scripture, faith, and tradition, or to change those opinions with the winds of fashionable opinion. Meanwhile, what is important is to have a redemptive approach to any situation or challenge in life. Keep a loving relationship with your children. The differences of opinion must be accepted on each side, which means that the parent must eventually allow the child to make his own decisions, while the child should continue to respect the opinions of his parents.

There is also the possibility that your child is unhappy with the prospect of living the homosexual life. He may be open to counseling with such groups as Exodus International, which seeks to treat homosexuality as a disorder to be lovingly healed. This is a controversial approach, of course, but there are still many psychiatrists and psychologists who view homosexuality not as a normal orientation but as a disorder to be treated.

Also consider seeking help and support for yourself. Counseling can help you work through some of the emotions you experience, and a good counselor can help you sort out all the issues on the way toward a healthy approach to a difficult situation. There are support groups for parents of homosexual and lesbian children in most cities today. It helps to know that someone else shares our struggles, and it's also beneficial to hear some of their ideas and perspectives.

LIVING TOGETHER

Our world now expects premarital sexual activity to the extent that chaste young people are looked upon as strange and old-fashioned. Teenagers are told that it is normal for them to be sexually active, and many of them feel pressured to follow that prophecy even though they are nervous and afraid and would rather wait until marriage. Even in many churches, we are meeting more and more couples who live together without being married. Young people feel that they can enjoy all the specific pleasures of marriage without taking on the responsibilities and burdens. Life is not that convenient, of course; many studies show that sexual promiscuity leads to unhappiness, and that marriages are even more likely to fail if the couple live together first. (The usual argument, of course, is that if a man and woman have a "trial cohabitation," they'll get a better idea of whether they're compatible; but it doesn't seem to work that way.)

> Many studies show that sexual promiscuity leads to unhappiness, and that marriages are even more likely to fail if the couple live together first.

What if your child mentions that he is living with a girlfriend? What if he wants to bring her to stay as a guest in your home, sharing his bedroom?

First, realize that there could be several underlying issues in such a situation. Once again, think about the anger factor. Young people with passive-aggressive anger will strike out at their parents through the very issues most likely to upset them—religion, sexuality, and personal appearance, for example. If this is your situation, then the whole point is to offend you. No amount of argument or explanation will make your child change his mind.

But it's entirely appropriate for you to be firm about the rules of your household. Be clear that people of opposite sexes don't stay together in your home, short of marriage. Any guest, even a family member, will need to respect the rules that every particular family observes. The "pleasant but firm" rule is so important here. Don't back down on your beliefs, but there's no need to be hostile either. Be loving, gentle, and insistent on what you feel is appropriate in the home your family has built. It's the best way to set an example for your child to follow.

Many parents are going to have to face these issues and others. There are simply times when we as parents have done all that we can do. Our children are not going to be carbon copies of us—unfortunately, even, at times, in issues that matter very much to us. We cannot endorse their behavior, but we can continue to love them and look for ways to redeem the situation and bring goodness out of it. For example, if you know your son is living with his girlfriend, you won't allow the two of them to sleep in the same bedroom; but does that mean she is unwelcome in your house at all? Of course not. This would be a poor way to win others to our faith and our convictions. When your son brings his girlfriend to visit, be pleasant, warm, and affectionate. Treat both of them as you would in any other situation, because you love your son *not* based on his actions measuring up to your expectations, but unconditionally.

> Any guest, even a family member, will need to respect the rules that every particular family observes.

Remember the example of Jesus, who socialized with everyone regardless of their personal morality. Never did he accept their actions, but he loved them in such a compelling way that it eventually *changed* their actions. Jesus still casts that powerful love over us, and he gives us the ability to love others in the same way. If you want your child to become spiritually, emotionally, and mentally mature, you must love him toward that goal rather than coercing him toward it. The best parents have discovered that it really works.

ten

SOUL PROVIDERS

On Sunday mornings we line the pews of our traditional churches. We listen to the organ begin its prelude, and the choir offers a call to worship. We sing the familiar old songs from the hymnal, the same songs our grandparents sang. We pass the offering plate and hear the kind of sermon we've always heard: a Bible reading, a joke, three practical points, and perhaps an altar call. The organ plays again, this time dismissing us to the challenges of our week.

As we stand and gather our belongings, considering whether to hit the cafeteria or the restaurant for Sunday dinner, we scan the sanctuary with our eyes. We see much the same crowd as usual; the same faces we've seen and known for years. The hair grows a little grayer with each passing week, there are a few more walking sticks and hearing aids, and just a few young parents in their thirties.

What we do *not* see is any significant accumulation of twenty-something worshippers. This is not a unique observation—there are more and more grumblings about the lack of young people in our churches, in fact. This is our congregation, and we are proud of it. How many times have we heard our preacher pronounce that "the church is only one generation away from extinction"? We get the point: if we don't reach younger people and school them in the faith, our church could be closing its doors in twenty years or less.

More about that later, but let's insert a little ray of sunshine right here. Amid all the moaning and groaning we are hearing about losing twenty-something believers from our churches, there is a separate trend that is very positive. All around us, young adults are worshipping and "doing church" without our realizing it. They're re-creating church in their own image, just as every generation has done. Many of us can remember when drums and guitars were absolutely forbidden in the sanctuary, before the baby boomers reached their teenage years and began to change worship as we know it. We survived the era of Christian music playing catch-up with cultural trends. Even our stodgiest old assemblies have slowly adapted and evolved more than most of us realize.

> The church is still changing and it must always change, in its superficial form. The important distinction is that the content of our faith *never* changes.

The church is still changing and it must always change, in its superficial form. The important distinction is that the content of our faith *never* changes. Jesus spoke of new wine and old wineskins. His word picture was that the drink itself was full of life, but the container was bound to wear out after a while and need replacing. We shouldn't be shocked when pipe organs give way to electronic keyboards and pews give way to theater seating.

It's true, as we'll see in the next section, that many twenty-some-things feel disconnected to the traditional church—the old hymns, the choirs and organs, and especially the committee and denominational politics. For many years it has actually been difficult to reach that age-group between twenty and thirty; married young adults tend to "nest" or to focus on building their homes before having a renewed interest in church when the children have arrived. But modern twenty-somethings aren't marrying. They aren't nesting but often returning to the old nest. And they are experiencing challenges and issues that, in their view, the church does not answer.

The issue of keeping your children connected on the path of faith (and by children, in this case I mean teenagers through young adults) is crucial. If the youth group in your church isn't vibrant, you're fighting a losing battle to get your teenager to contribute; if there are no young adults, it's the same with your twenty-some-thing son or daughter. In the latter case, our children might as well find some church that does meet their needs, and you may have to encourage them to begin the search. Even though you love your congregation, and even though your child may have grown up there and may be among the people that love him, he needs to be in a place where he can truly connect and become involved.

> The bottom line is that if our children are going to carry on the faith that means so much to us, we can't assume it will happen naturally.

A few churches are doing a good job with this age-group—mostly larger churches that are growth-oriented and have a particular vision for reaching young adults. It takes a lot of commitment, work, and special resources to get that job done. You need leadership that understands the needs of twenty-somethings; gifted communicators and musicians who fit the need; and very often, a unique place to meet. Twenty-somethings tend to enjoy using nontraditional worship spaces, so churches are renting space in shopping centers, business complexes, or other surroundings.

Some churches simply aren't willing to go to that much trouble when their present membership keeps them busy with its needs. And of course, most churches lack those special resources. The bottom line is that if our children are going to carry on the faith that means so much to us, we can't assume it will happen naturally. We need to be proactive in ministering to twenty-somethings with the old, cherished, and unchanged faith, but through new, vibrant strategies.

Meanwhile, we must discard the assumption that these twenty-somethings aren't reachable—that they are too worldly, too self-absorbed, or simply nonspiritual.

Let's discover some fresh findings about the spirituality of this generation.

A HUNGRY GENERATION

In 2000, journalist Colleen Carroll began a study of young adults and their attraction to the traditional doctrines of Christianity. The Phillips Foundation Journalism Fellowship Program awarded her a $50,000 grant, and Carroll interviewed more than five hundred young adults. Her resulting book was called *The New Faithful: Why Young Adults Are Embracing Christian Orthodoxy*.

What surprised the author most was how widespread she found this movement to be. She found a tremendous number of twenty-somethings who are moving toward essential Christianity, though often in new forms. She discovered that there were so many young people who wanted to tell her their stories, she didn't have time for them all—a rare experience in journalism. Obviously she had touched a nerve.

Why are twenty-somethings turning to faith? In an interview with *Christianity Today*, Colleen Carroll said:

> In general, there is a reaction against the larger culture—a feeling of being saturated by greed, sex, and all the decadent forces in our culture. But sociology is not the full explanation here. There is a deep spiritual hunger that transcends sociology.[1]

She believes that young people feel an emptiness from life and the world around them as they have found it so far. So many more of them have seen the pain of divorce in their families. They have also experienced the contagions of materialism, greed, and sensuality in our culture. In such times, the appeal of faith always becomes stronger and more attractive. There is a powerful cynicism in our entertainment, our news commentary, and everything we produce as a culture. A great nihilism (an extreme skepticism that denies any true meaning in life) pervades our world, and each generation of young people brings an idealism with them. They reject the prospect of a hedonistic world where there is nothing to hold on to but momentary pleasure. They want ultimate answers, and in particular they want to give their time and their efforts to meaningful service.

> This is the first generation in a long time for which faith requires a deliberate decision.

Carroll points out that this is the first generation in a long time for which faith requires a deliberate decision. She wrote, "It's not something embedded in their family anymore."[2] And this is true. Many of their parents dropped out of church in their own young adult years and have yet to return. We live in a post-Christian society by and large, where the common biblical values and ideas cannot be taken for granted in the man or woman on the street. Twenty-somethings live in a world where faith is much less common than agnosticism or atheism. Therefore, if they decide to be true seekers of God, they must make a serious decision to do so. No cheap faith or "easy-believism" will do for many young people of this generation; if they're going to commit themselves to Christianity or some other faith, they're going to be very serious about it.

This new breed of Christian young adult is reacting against such trends as the sexual promiscuity of our time.

We've also alluded to the fact that active service is a strong component of young adult faith. It makes sense, of course, that young people are energetic and want to be actively involved. It's also a reaction against a church that has shirked some of its social responsibilities, in their view. Seeing problems in the city, they want to make a greater difference. Seeing our nation less popular abroad, they want to go and light a candle so others won't curse the darkness.

It's also hopeful to learn that this new breed of Christian young adult is reacting against such trends as the sexual promiscuity of our time. As a matter of fact, recent college polls seem to suggest that approval of premarital sex is on the decrease rather than the increase. Again, younger believers see themselves as having made a significant choice in life; they don't shy away from the behavioral implications of that choice.

Another trend is that among younger adults, "brand names"

(denominations) are far less meaningful. On many college campuses, Catholics and Protestants not only worship together, but they learn from each other. Those who have been raised as Baptists may long for the "high," dignified worship of Catholics or Episcopalians; they embrace the Catholic Eucharist. Roman Catholics, meanwhile, are attracted to the devout evangelical zeal and contemporary worship of some of their Protestant friends. There has been a healthy crossover in both directions.

UNREACHED TWENTY-SOMETHINGS

Worthy of note is that Colleen Carroll's encouraging research was directed toward the significant number of twenty-somethings who are "within the fold," so to speak. Unfortunately, the church can't conclude that it is in good shape with this generation as a whole—only that there is a healthy trend of twenty-something Christianity.

George Barna, the pollster who is the founder of the Barna Group, a market research organization, has also studied the faith habits of twenty-somethings. After carefully interviewing 2,660 young adults, he published a report on the generation as a whole. Not surprisingly, his take is a bit more unsettling. Barna concluded that:

> Americans in their twenties are significantly less likely than any other age group to attend church services, to donate to churches, to be absolutely committed to Christianity, to read the Bible, or to serve as a volunteer or lay leader in churches.[3]

Barna offers the figures that only three of every ten twenty-somethings attend church in a typical week. By comparison, four of ten thirty-somethings do so, and five of ten forty-somethings are found in the pews during a typical week.

Not only that, but we can't blame this widespread dropout on the college years—at least not completely. The worst attendance figures were found among the older twenty-somethings, who had been out of school for the longest period. Barna's conclusion is that between ages eighteen and twenty-nine, our population shows a 58 percent attendance drop. Yet 80 percent of our twenty-somethings say that religious faith is very important to them.[4]

So we have looked at those young adults who are recommitting themselves to classic Christianity and reshaping the church. We have then taken a darker look at the churchgoing habits of the generation as a whole. The conclusion is a mixed one. Christianity will not become extinct anytime soon, since millions of young adults not only attend church but are very devout in their faith. On the other hand, the future promises to be dominated on a cultural level by nonbelievers, unless we see a major spiritual revival such as those that occurred in past centuries.

> The future promises to be dominated on a cultural level by nonbelievers, unless we see a major spiritual revival such as those that occurred in past centuries.

What about your own child? In which category does she take her stand? Is she one of the "new faithful," boldly going where no Christian has gone before? Or is she a lapsed believer or perhaps not a believer at all? Is she somewhere in the middle, still trying to decide her identity?

Either way, your own faith may be the most powerful spiritual influence in her life. Given such a difficult and personal topic, what can you do to guide her toward a powerful, sustaining faith?

A FAITH TO FOLLOW

First, we should mention what you should not do. Don't nag your child or use guilt to get her to go to church when her heart isn't in it. This suggestion sounds obvious enough, but it's a difficult rule to follow, wouldn't you agree? We notice our young adult children sleeping late on Sunday mornings. We observe that their friends are drawn from a group that is obviously not devoted to our faith. Sometimes it seems hard not to ask, "Why don't you attend church with us anymore? You know it's good for you. Don't you worry about displeasing God?"

That approach will get exactly the response you expect. While it's hard to sit by and watch her drift away from the life patterns by which you've raised her, you need to think carefully (and pray a lot) about your approach. Here are some positive strategies:

PRACTICE A POSITIVE FAITH

It's easier said than done, but this is by far your most important priority if you want your children to think more about faith issues. Twenty-somethings are often reacting against the practice of a religion that to them seems insincere and irrelevant. How can your child see the impact of faith in your life? Do you share with your family decisions that are motivated by your commitment to Christ? Do you get involved with church service and mission projects? What about the place of prayer in your home? Do you tell each member of your family, on a regular basis, how you're praying for each of them specifically? Are you "caught" studying the Bible during your free time?

Another point of contention is how we as adults relate to the church. If your adult child has observed that you come home complaining about church leadership or gossiping about the members, this helps to make church involvement very unattractive to a younger person. Of course we must acknowledge that being integrally involved in a church can be a messy business; we do have conflicts with leaders and other members, and it's impossible not to bring some of that home. Just the same, your young adult needs to see a largely positive and rewarding view of the impact of the church on your life. She needs to understand the distinction that the church is not perfect, but that it is in every way worth the investment of time and tears we give it.

For example, make a point of showing your adult child how church members care for one another in times of crisis. This is often one of the shining moments for the local fellowship: when you're in the hospital and members come visit you, or when you have a job crisis and everyone gathers around to offer support. Twenty-somethings are searching for close and meaningful community, and your task is to show your child that there is no fellowship more satisfying than the church. In this regard, you'll need to take the lead in being that kind of member yourself. Visit an ailing friend and take your child along, or ask for your child to accompany you on a missions project.

> Have you ever told your children how you became a believer, and the difference it made in your life?

MAKE USE OF YOUR TESTIMONY

It has been said that skeptics can lodge their arguments about every doctrinal point of our faith, but they can't take away our personal experience. Have you ever told your children how you became a believer, and the difference it made in your life? Do you make regular reference to this experience in order to underline the fact that this major turning point in your life continues to be significant? A good way to polish your testimony is to write it down. I would recommend that every parent make a carefully written record of their testimony (along with childhood memories and other significant pieces of the past) as a legacy for their children. Would you know how to go about it, other than telling where you walked down the aisle of a church and when? The outline of a strong testimony is as follows:

    I. My life before I came to faith
   II. How I came to faith
  III. The difference in my life since I came to faith

Notice that you don't need a dramatic narrative. The actual events may be very mundane. But you should be able to detail the difference that your faith has made in your life. Find a casual and spontaneous (nonpreachy) moment to speak about where you were in your faith as a twenty-something yourself. Most of us, of course, still had a long way to go in terms of wisdom at that age. Your story will help your twenty-something see that you've been where she is now; she'll grasp the greater perspective of her place in life, and your experiences may suggest to her that a legitimate and highly significant part of her journey is the journey of faith.

USE DAILY CONVERSATION

As you and your adult child discuss the events of a typical day, find places to lightly give reference to God's part in things. Many twenty-somethings (and many of the rest of us) connect God to only the big decisions: whom to marry, where to work, and so on.

As you "practice the presence of God" in your own daily life, you can show your adult child how you do that and how God's companionship makes a wonderful difference, particularly in the most troubled times.

At the same time, avoid offering the picture of a parent who has all the answers, spiritual and otherwise. Your child won't buy it. Remember, young people have special antennae for detecting hypocrisy. Always be real. Make a great point to share your struggles in faith, talking about your answered prayers as well as your unanswered ones. What you want to pass on to your children is the picture of an authentic faith, and the life of faith is never perfect or easy. In the New Testament we find this truth:

> Young people have special antennae for detecting hypocrisy. Always be real.

Consider it pure joy, my brothers, whenever you face trials of many kinds, because you know that the testing of your faith develops perseverance. Perseverance must finish its work so that you may be mature and complete, not lacking anything. (James 1:2–4)

When life takes a left turn for you or your family, a doubting twenty-something may be thinking, *Where is their God now? What difference does it make to be a believer anyway?* In these troubled times, faith doesn't crumble; it stands in powerful testimony. You have an opportunity to discuss how God is teaching you patience or perseverance through every trial. You can show that God isn't absent when things go wrong; on the contrary, we feel his presence more clearly than ever.

These lessons in the midst of life will go a long way toward molding the faith of your children.

HELP FIND A GOOD CHURCH

It's terrific when you have a church that every member of your family can attend together. I believe families should worship together as part of the same body of faith. In this day of change, however, that's not always realistic. If your church has no significant ministry to offer to young adults, you need to help your adult child realize that there could be a much more meaningful worship, fellowship, and service experience elsewhere.

You may find that she is eager to attend services with you during traditional times of the year—Christmas and Easter—because young people still resonate with the traditions of their childhood, and they long to reexperience that special feeling they had while sitting with you in the pew. Take advantage of those Christmas vesper services and special programs of Easter music. They may feel the call of God at these events. On the whole, however, they seem not to feel that week by week, the "old-school" church will have anything to offer.

The average twenty-something, of course, will not be proactive in switching churches; she will simply drop out when the Sunday experience stops connecting with her. You may want to take that burden, but you will want to do it discretely. Don't make a great point of shopping for fellowships for your child; your child will feel pressured. And we do want our children to stand on their own feet, make their own decisions, and chart their own courses. But this is a special case—you don't want your adult child to drift into just any belief system. Better that you know the spiritual landscape of your city or town, and do your research. In a moment I'll have more to say about that point.

> We all need to encourage the leadership of our church to be more proactive in reaching young adults.

PUSH FOR IMPROVEMENT AT YOUR CHURCH

We all need to encourage the leadership of our church to be more proactive in reaching young adults. Most churches give lip service to this idea, but we find out the truth if we take a quick look at the budget and the work assignments of the ministerial staff. The church that truly wants to make a difference with young adults won't simply be talking about it, but doing something about it. It will be establishing worship services in the style that appeals to this generation. It will be hiring staff who know how to get the job done, and creating programs that minister to the needs of twenty-somethings.

You can help your church staff do this. Sometimes the problem is that "the squeaky wheel gets the grease." The pastor and his staff have their arms full with the needs and demands of an aging membership. It's very difficult to be in the field of professional ministry today because, to put it bluntly, many of us are too hard on our ministers. We demand all their time, we bring our anger from elsewhere to church, and we quickly discard ministers if we find something wrong with them. So many of them are struggling just to survive; how are they supposed to be starting creative new ministries?

Laypeople need to provide the energy and the momentum for reaching young adults. We need to support our staff as new services and programs are added. We need to provide the financial and other resources needed. And we need to have a better vision of the future of our particular church, because if we don't reach these young adults, it may be that there is no future.

HELP THEM ASK THE RIGHT QUESTIONS

Your daughter is having dinner at your home. You ask her what is new in her world, and she tells you she's gotten involved with a church across town. Well, that's good news! You want to know all about it, so you ask her to fill you in.

She tells you the basics: where this new worship center can be found, what kind of music and message can be heard there, and, of course, the fact that a lot of other guys and girls her age are in attendance.

You ask, "What denomination is it?"

She vaguely says, "I don't know, really. There is no denomination in the name. It's just called 'The Believers' Gathering.'"

You say, "I see. Well, what are the core beliefs?"

Again, she hesitates. "I haven't really picked up on anything like that. They just talk and sing about God and they do a lot of service projects. Worship is cool, really casual with a hot band. You know, that kind of church."

I have noticed that many of these new churches for twenty-somethings are springing up, and many of them are fine, biblical churches—new wine in new wineskins. Just the same, there's reason for concern because young people can be very naive about drifting into these organizations. They make their decisions based on the exterior experience rather than the interior doctrinal framework. Some of these assemblies are growing quickly and taking in a great deal of money. But with a little investigative work we discover that the leaders have no accountability (denominational or otherwise), and in some cases, their doctrine is more deviant than most of the members realize.

Quite controversial, for example, is the Emerging Church movement, which focuses on twenty-somethings. It is heavily influenced by postmodern philosophy, including the proposition that absolute truth cannot be known, and that therefore doctrine is less important than personal experience. Leadership in this exploding movement is decentralized and often unaccountable. Totally uninhibited leadership plus loosened doctrine is obviously a troubling combination. On the other hand, the traditional church can learn certain important lessons from this model, particularly in how to win the hearts of young adults. The new, younger forms of church often have powerful fellowship and effective community service.

This is just an example of why we need to help our young adults be wise and discerning as they find a forum for the journey of their faith. How can you help? First of all, do your homework. Find out what is available in your area so that you'll have the background knowledge—and possibly make an alternate recommendation if your child strays in a dangerous direction. As for the new young and mysterious congregation in your midst, get the best facts you can. But never attack it in the presence of your child. It's highly counterproductive to create a point of tension over this decision.

It's a much better strategy to pleasantly ask questions. Tell me about this new church? Who is the pastor? Who holds him or her accountable? What are the core beliefs? When you find that your young adult child knows less than you do about the basics, suggest that you go to the computer together and check the church's Web site—not confrontationally but "just for the information." Most young adult churches will certainly have a Web site in this day and age, because young adults get information on virtually everything through the Internet. Alternatively, your child can ask for a printed statement of faith.

Study that statement carefully with your child. As for hierarchy and accountability, you may need to encourage your child to ask some questions. "Do you know where your money is going? Does the church make its accounting books public?"

What you're doing is teaching your child to be as wise as a serpent while remaining as innocent as a dove. Demonstrate to her the kind of questions she should be asking, and teach her to tread very carefully in the places in life where it is easy to be taken advantage of. If your young adult child has a disheartening experience with some new form of church, it can have the effect of hardening her heart against churches in the future. As always, it's a great idea to keep the channels of dialogue open. If you express your unconditional love to your child in the right ways and maintain a positive relationship, she will come to you with information about all of the important developments in her life. You'll be able to casually converse with her in a way that trains her even while she probably doesn't realize she is gaining the wisdom of your lifetime experience.

BE HOPEFUL

Even before this present generation, we knew that young adults were likely to leave the church for a season. As young single adults, they have found in the past that the church is all about families and older people. Only in recent years has it become common to find single adult ministry in larger churches.

> If you have raised her in a healthy spiritual environment, you've planted the seed. Ultimately that's the most we can really do.

Even so, twenty-somethings continue to leave the church, enjoy their youth, sleep late on Sundays, get married, and return to church for the spiritual education of their children. It simply seems to be part of the American pattern. If your adult child shows no interest in spirituality for the time being, or at least shows no interest in organized religion, then you should not panic.

Step back and give her the space she needs to work through her own approach to God, even as you continue to use the positive strategies we've already mentioned.

Give your adult child some benefit of the doubt. If you have raised her in a healthy spiritual environment, you've planted the seed. Ultimately that's the most we can really do. Every adult must finally establish his or her own faith; it cannot be tangibly inherited like a golden pocket watch or a sum of money. Your child will ask the questions all of us ask, and she will find her own way. Have faith that she finds the God you have shown her in the past.

> Love brings out the best in us concerning those we care about; "It always protects, always trusts, always hopes, always perseveres" (1 Cor. 13:7).

Finally, trust in God himself. He is the one who loves us with an everlasting love. He loves your child just as you love her—the way he loves each of us. And he calls to us patiently, with long-suffering, and his love and grace continue to await us, no matter how far we roam from his presence.

He is like the father in Jesus's story of the prodigal son. That son may well have been a twenty-something; we usually picture him that way. He wandered off into a life not too different from the decadent life of many young people today. He seemed much more interested in parties and good times than in the traditions of his family. In every way, he seemed to renounce his birthright, his family's good name, and everything his father had labored to teach him.

Did the father grow bitter? Did he say, "I have no son from here on"? Not at all. Instead he went on with his life, but with an eye on the road that led home. He watched and waited for his son to return to the fold, never giving up hope that it would happen.

And when that son did appear, sadder but wiser, the father wrapped his arms around him in joy, threw a great party, and it was as if the young man had never left.

There's a lesson in that story for all of us who worry about the fate of our children. Love does worry sometimes; it comes with the territory. But love brings out the best in us concerning those we care about; "It always protects, always trusts, always hopes, always perseveres" (1 Cor. 13:7).

As you love God and love your child, have faith that you can be some part of the bridge between them. And if not, trust God alone. He is calling to your child, and his voice is very hard to resist when heard amid the pain and confusion of today's world.

eleven

WAITING FOR THE FUTURE

You're walking along a beautiful beach at sunrise. You drink in the quiet dignity of the hour, well before the vacationers have taken control of the area. You enjoy the arc of the seagulls in the sky, the slap of the surf against the sand, and everything else about this hour and this shore.

There's something about a quiet walk at the beach that separates us from the hustle and bustle of the moment. In the face of nature's power, our problems don't seem so all-conquering. For that matter, we don't feel so all-important either. After all, we look at the relentless waves, pounding and pounding against the shore. How many centuries, how many millennia have they gone about their work? How many more, after we are gone? Beside this ocean, it is possible to feel very inconsequential.

You stop and turn around for a moment, studying the footprints of your bare feet along the beach. The rising tide is already wearing them away. Only those imprints from the last moment or two remain, and in a few brief seconds, they will be washed away as well.

Such is the legacy of a life. As the years pass you by, the speed of time seems to increase, and there's nothing anyone can do to slow it down. At midlife, you want to stop and reflect, to take stock while there is still a chance. You try to think of some way you can make those footprints deeper, longer lasting, more resistant to the pounding of that unrelenting sea.

You wonder again whether you will be remembered one hundred years from today. In the New Testament, James wrote, "Why, you do not even know what will happen tomorrow. What is your life? You are a mist that appears for a little while and then vanishes" (James 4:14). What a Bible verse—not exactly encouraging, is it? You and I definitely want to see our lives as something more than vapor that vanishes in the air. How can you reach forward into the future? What does it take for us to know we have made a deep impression in the shifting sands of this world?

There are a couple of ways. For one, we can give ourselves to causes that matter. Through our work and our giving, we can create a legacy that continues to act on our behalf long after we are gone. Bill and Melinda Gates, for example, have created a charitable foundation to provide life-saving healthcare products and technology to the poorest parts of the world. Henry Ford created the Ford Foundation, James B. Duke created the Duke Endowment, and many other wealthy and celebrated figures have done the same. Even with the impact these tycoons achieved through their own businesses, they realized there was only one way for their work to live on.

> What does it take for us to know we have made a deep impression in the shifting sands of this world?

"That's inspiring," you answer before sighing deeply. "But I don't have hundreds of millions of dollars. I don't have a vision for solving world hunger or curing cancer or even taking the gospel to the ends of the earth. Certainly I'll contribute to all of those causes—but I want to have a *personal* impact, know what I mean?"

Yes, we understand. And indeed there's another way for us to create a lasting legacy. It doesn't have much to do with funding; it's made of a contribution more valuable than mere money. That contribution, of course, is our children.

You may have already taken some steps toward your children's legacy. You did so if you helped them get an education. You may also have kept your legal will updated, in order to designate what property will go to which child. Some parts of your legacy are simply built-in: your child's distinctive laugh from his mother's side of the family; his quick wit from the father's side; this or that facial feature, athletic ability, or personality trait. Someday, after you're gone, a relative or an old family friend will look into the eyes of your child and say, "I see your mother (or your father) in you."

And so, in that way, you will live on in a very personal way. And as your children build families of their own, your DNA will climb down the ladder of time into the future.

THE LEGACY OF CHARACTER

The most important parts of your legacy, in my belief, have nothing to do with eye color or musical talent or any of those other inborn traits. They don't concern your Christmas rituals, your dinnertime traditions, or any of those other habits that are dispersed into the world like a mist on the summer wind. I believe that the hallmarks of character and integrity are your greatest legacy.

Think of the power of the moral lessons you have taught. You are driving along with your younger child in the car. Pulling out of a shopping center, you don't have quite enough room to turn, and you slightly dent the expensive sports car next to you. It's a busy day, there are a thousand things on your mind, and it would be so easy to simply drive away, leaving the dented sports car without explanation. But you know what is right. And so you pull back into the space, park your car, and wait for the other driver to return. When he does, you apologize and point to the dent. You offer your personal information, including auto insurance, to the slightly irritated sports car driver.

> I believe that the hallmarks of character and integrity are your greatest legacy.

It's no momentous event in the life of your family. But a child is watching. At this very moment, you have contributed to his legacy in the world. And another way to look at it is that you have just made the future a slightly more honest, slightly more civil time. Your son, you see, is highly likely to handle situations just as he has seen you handle them.

At home, you read books of history for personal enlightenment. You study your Bible and take an interest in current events. Your child is watching again. He sees the joy you take in bettering yourself and getting involved with your world, and he begins to place a value in those things.

Someone comes to the door collecting money right in the middle of dinner. Your child sees that you're a bit annoyed, but he also sees how you refuse to expend that emotion on the visitor, who is collecting money for a Boy Scout project. You pull some money out of your wallet, but you also stop to ask questions about the project, offering encouragement and shaking the visitor's hand. Young eyes watch every move, every testament of simple grace and generosity.

Then, when a neighbor, chatting over the fence, offers a slight racial slur in the midst of a conversation, your child notices that your expression becomes blank for a second, your eyes a bit hard. At the first opportunity, you lead him inside the house, point out the slur, and explain why negative racial remarks are never appropriate and never tolerable. Not only does your child hear your words, but something more important happens: He sees your emotion. He sees that this is an issue that matters to you, so it must be significant. And you have just created a small legacy of positive racial relations in our future.

> If your twenty-something has stalled in the direction of his life, how powerful is the influence of his family that hasn't?

And never, during any of these events, did you think of your actions this way. But now your child is in his twenties. It's easy to believe that those influential times are over, and that he finds his models for living elsewhere. He certainly doesn't wear his clothing or hair the way you raised him. He watches different shows, listens to different music, and has interests that are all his own. And he chooses to spend his time elsewhere, with his friends. That's the way things usually work out, of course. He is becoming his own person.

But you are still leaving a legacy. We've pointed it out all through this book. Every time you discuss matters of faith or of friendship, every time you talk about the pros and cons of certain career choices, and every time you speak of any other subject, for that matter, you are still making small contributions to a legacy that is far greater than your savings account or your beach house or your father's golden watch-chain.

As a matter of fact, now is the time you can make a highly significant impression. If your twenty-something has stalled in the direction of his life, how powerful is the influence of his family that hasn't? If you find joy and direction through prayer and church life, won't the message come across to someone who needs joy and direction? If you are involved in missions trips and service projects, won't your child be more proud of you and be more likely to remember that gracious service is a vital part of life?

Your marriage, too, is important. If you have a spouse, your pattern of loving interaction is creating a pattern that is likely to be followed. If you are single through divorce or loss, the way you handle that challenge is highly significant to your children as well.

THE LEGACY OF LOVE

Most of all, there is the legacy of love. There are only a few items mentioned in Scripture that are eternal: God, people, God's Word, his law, and love. Paul says that faith, hope, and love are things that remain—but the greatest of all is love (1 Cor. 13:13). It is the only trait identified with God in a completely direct correspondence: "God is love" (1 John 4:8). That should tell us that love is the most powerful force in the universe. It casts out all darkness, it heals all grief, and it gives meaning to the loneliest moment.

You have this time, this twilight of adolescence before the onset of adulthood, to continue loving your twenty-something child. Yes, you have loved him since birth; even before that. You would give your life for him, because that's the way God made parents. Ask nearly any mother or father the question, and they would tell you in a heartbeat that they would do for their child what God did for all of us—give their life.

Here is my question for you: If you love him enough to die for him, can you love him enough to live for him?

The truth is that you have these years to live and to love your adult child. If you offer unconditional love, you are endowing him with a power and a potential that nothing else in life can give him. And without it, he will find his life very difficult to bear. Even now, as he tries to figure out the next steps in his pathway, he is emboldened and empowered by knowing that behind and beneath him is an unquestionable foundation of parental love. He can attempt great things, and your love follows him. He can utterly fail, and your love follows him still, providing consolation and new strength.

The central work of parenting may well be done. He has learned to walk, to speak, to read and write, to move about socially, to educate and care for himself, and all the basics of life. Think of today as the "polishing years." The raw material is there, but a great deal of burnishing, glazing, and smoothing still needs to be done. Sometimes this is the most important work of all.

Michelangelo was the greatest sculptor of the Italian Renaissance. He would devote several years, a great section of his life, to some particular commissioned statue: *David* or the *Piéta* or an angel for the pope's tomb. Knowing how intimately he would be involved with one block of marble, the artist traveled to the quarry to supervise the mining and selection of the block. He studied every layer of rock carefully before finally choosing the great cube of marble on which his hands would soon labor with the subtle initiative of genius. Michelangelo understood that there

> If you offer unconditional love, you are endowing him with a power and a potential that nothing else in life can give him.

was no unflawed stone. He sought the purest but knew that his craft was to make the flaws invisible.

The artist would begin his sculpting with the hammer and the chisel. First he would pound away, knocking off the corners and the outer layers that would not be needed. Then he would work over the profile with the fine point of his chisel. Very slowly, over days and months and years, as the seasons came and went, a work of breathtaking and immortal beauty would emerge from what was once an impassive block of stone.

Someone asked Michelangelo about his secret. How could he create figures made from marble, but so lifelike that you almost hear the heartbeat and feel the pulse?

Michelangelo replied that there was no secret; the process was simple, really. His simple calling was to take a stone and liberate the angel within it. It was simply his job to chip away and remove everything that was not the angel.

Isn't that something like the job you're accomplishing now? The hammering years are gone, and sometimes those were quite painful. But there is still some fine detail-work left to complete. You must chip away, gently, lovingly, and never stop working the stone until an angel has emerged.

> You must chip away, gently, lovingly, and never stop working the stone until an angel has emerged.

A VISION OF POTENTIAL

Your child may be no angel, but he is an immortal creature; God has promised that every single one of us bears that distinction. Your twenty-something is created in the image not only of his earthly parents but of his heavenly one. Your best gift is to chisel with love so that he doesn't even know he is being sculpted, and to work with a mental picture of the angel that someday he can be; to imagine the immortal child of God that he was brought into this world to become. Love ignores the flaws and sees the possibilities, and it stubbornly works until those possibilities completely cover the flaws.

Give him your love, and give it lavishly, even when you're tired, a little frustrated, and a little doubtful whether the angel is going to emerge at all. In Paul's words, always protect, always trust, always hope, always persevere (1 Cor. 13:7).

And someday, when your years on this earth have drawn to a close, he will surely and boldly stand on his own two feet. He, in turn, will begin the work of leaving his own legacy with those who come behind him—and on and on the process will continue, until the book of time itself reaches its final page. Then, in the next life, you and your child will be united once more. Can you imagine the greatness, the fullness, the soul-deep joy of that day? Your son will walk up to you and embrace you with laughter. He will say, "Now I know how deep your love for me was. Now I understand the countless ways you planted the seeds of your life, your honesty, your godliness in me. I wish you could have seen the work and the good things that came to pass in my life, and in the lives of others, simply because of the way you loved me. Because one seed bears many sprouts."

And then he'll stand aside, and you'll see the throng of people who have accompanied him on their journey to thank you—

> Love ignores the flaws and sees the possibilities, and it stubbornly works until those possibilities completely cover the flaws.

people of all kinds, people of all colors, all touched by the long chain of which you were one willing link; the chain that we call human legacy.

Yes, love is the world's most powerful force. The financial endowments will pass away; the antique furniture will one day be no more. But the greatest of these is love. Give it now, give it freely, and it will take root in your children, your world, and the world's future. This is my prayer for you as the parent of an adult child. May God help you fulfill the prayer and find joy in the outcome.

FIVE WAYS TO GET THE MOST FROM THIS BOOK

1. AROUND TOWN

Do you know other parents of twenty-somethings in your area? Invite them to come to your home for a weekly discussion over coffee while you discuss the book chapter by chapter. You'll enjoy building relationships on your street—and when the study is complete, your friends will find they've become a parental support group for advice and encouragement.

2. OVER THE WEEKEND

Have a "Twenty-Something Parent Getaway" as a weekend retreat. Hit the book's key points for group sessions, small-group interaction, and a closing time of prayer and commitment. A concentrated weekend focus on the material will give it extra impact, and you'll come home refreshed and rejuvenated, ready to apply your new understandings.

3. IN THE CLASSROOM

Study a chapter per week with your adult Sunday school class. *Help Your Twenty-Something Get a Life . . . and Get it Now* can become a practical and rewarding class curriculum. Class members will enjoy comparing notes from their parenting experiences during the week—and reporting the week's progress in applying what they learn.

4. WITH YOUR SPOUSE

For a very personal one-on-one study experience, study each chapter of this book with your spouse. Plan and protect an uninterrupted hour once or twice per week for reviewing the chapters and applying them to your household's special challenges. You'll grow together as a couple even as you grow into wiser parenthood.

5. OVER THE INTERNET

Start a "Twenty-Something Parenting" bulletin board (such as a Google group or Yahoo group), and invite your friends to log on and share insights as they work through the book. Long after your study is finished, parents will want to continue sharing their experiences and assistance in your Web group.

{study guide}

Use this special chapter-by-chapter guide to enhance your growth as a parent. The questions are designed in such a way that you can use them in your personal study, in discussion with your spouse, or in a more formal group learning experience.

Note the three kinds of questions provided:

1. START.

The first question for each chapter is a general (and gentle) way to begin thinking about the chapter's topic. It will help you or your group recall personal experiences that relate to the main subject of our discussion. In a group session, this question is a good "ice-breaker"—that is, it makes it easy for participants to jump right into the session.

2. STUDY.

These questions—five or more of them—move you through the main points of each chapter. Their goal is not only to help you clarify the key ideas, but to begin thinking about how they will help you as a parent.

3. STRENGTHEN.

Each chapter's final question will motivate you to consider how to put these truths to work during the next few days. These may be the most important questions of all, so if you study this book in a group setting, be certain you leave enough time to discuss the *strengthen* question.

{1} A GENERATIONAL PROFILE

START

1. Think about your years between ages twenty and thirty. How were they different from the experience of your son or daughter?

STUDY

1. How would you compare your generation to the one that produced your child?
2. What impact has the difference made upon your job as a parent?
3. Identify some of the financial challenges that twenty-somethings face.
4. Why is this an age of fear for young adults?
5. What is meant by a "nonlinear" approach to life? How does that description apply (or not) to your child?

STRENGTHEN

1. List or describe your current three greatest concerns about parenting your young adult child. What was the most helpful fact about the generation that you learned from this chapter?

{2} MATURE ADULTS ONLY

START

1. What is your personal definition of adulthood?
   How can you tell when your child has become
   an adult?

STUDY

1. What modern developments have blurred the distinctions
   between adolescence and adulthood?
2. Study the chart that illustrates Natalie's development. What
   would a chart look like for your child?
3. How have changes in our cultural climate affected the
   maturity of our children?
4. What does integrity have to do with adulthood? How can it
   be measured?
5. Describe the marks of emotional maturity. Which do you
   think is the most important?

STRENGTHEN

1. Given the descriptions of maturity in this chapter,
   how would you describe your adult child's current
   standing? In what ways does he seem most mature?
   In what ways least?

{3} BACK TO BASICS

START

1. In the past, how would you have described the basics of
   parenting?

STUDY

1. What are the four basic areas of parenting as defined by Dr. Campbell? Which do you think is most important, and why?
2. What are the most effective ways to express love to a young adult?
3. What are the greatest challenges of discipline for a twenty-something child?
4. Can you still protect an adult child from harmful influences? If so, what are the best ways?
5. Why is anger such a particular danger in today's world? How do you see it in the life of your child?

STRENGTHEN

1. Draw four columns on a sheet of paper. Devote each to one of the four basic areas of parenting. Based on your study of this chapter, list ideas in each column for improving your parenting in that area.

{4} WHEN JOHNNY COMES MARCHING HOME

START

1. What is the greatest challenge of having a twenty-something at home from the parent's perspective, in your opinion? From the young adult's perspective?

STUDY

1. What are the differences between "delaying" and "retreating"?
2. Why are practical planning sessions so important? Why do many parents tend to avoid them?

3. What are the most important points to discuss before your child moves home?
4. What is a good time frame for allowing an adult child to live at home, in your opinion?
5. What are some good ways to keep a positive frame of mind during this challenge?

STRENGTHEN

1. What practical step can you take this week to improve your relationship with your child, whether or not he or she lives at home?

{5} CARING FOR YOU

START

1. Dr. Campbell observes that, in his opinion, "people will not take care of themselves these days." Thinking about your age-group, why do you agree or disagree?

STUDY

1. What are the most important physical aspects of self-care?
2. How can you better tend to your emotional health?
3. Have you considered spirituality to be a health matter in the past? What can you do to care for yourself in this area?
4. What are some practical ways to get help from your personal support community?
5. Considering body, spirit, and emotions, which

represents your greatest need for care? How can you
meet that need?

STRENGTHEN

1. To repeat Dr. Campbell's question at the close of this
   chapter, are you up to the task of parenting an adult child?
   Defend your answer.

{6} MIND, MOOD, AND MEDS

START

1. How would you summarize your adult child's emotional
   health at present?

STUDY

1. Why do we tend to overemphasize an adult child's
   superficial life circumstances while underemphasizing
   the emotional ones?
2. Describe the so-called "quarterlife crisis."
3. What is the best way to help a young adult with anxiety?
   What about depression?
4. Substance abuse is a significant problem among
   young adults. How can we help them conquer it?
5. Should materialism be considered with the other problems
   in this chapter? Why or why not?

STRENGTHEN

1. What is your adult child's most significant emotional
   challenge? What is the most important practical step
   you can take to help your child?

{7} CASH, CREDIT, AND CHARACTER

START

1. Why is money management such a prominent problem between these two particular generations (baby boomer parents, current young adults)?

STUDY

1. What are some differences in the ways that parents and children tend to think of financial resources?
2. How do young adults often manipulate their parents to gain the things they want?
3. Why is the phrase "pleasant but firm" so important?
4. What can a parent do to help a young adult child manage his or her own earned money?
5. What are the crucial steps that young adults can consider in setting financial goals?

STRENGTHEN

1. How does your child relate to money? What can you do to help train him or her in this area?

{8} JOB ONE: ONE JOB

START

1. What are some distinctives in the ways that twenty-somethings approach the job market?

STUDY

1. What is a McJob?
2. What classic mistake do many young adults make when they gravitate toward recreation or hobby-related jobs?
3. What are some good tips for talking to our young adult children about the subject of careers?
4. Beyond the necessity for money, why is work so important in the life of adults? What is the biblical concept of our relationship to work?
5. What are some good ways a young adult can discover the most appropriate career?

STRENGTHEN

1. How does your own child relate to the subject of work? What should you do this week to help?

{9} DATING AND RELATING

START

1. Why are so many young adults delaying marriage?

STUDY

1. Why is the emphasis on soul mates so important to young adults?
2. What practical perspectives do young adults need to discover about marriage?
3. How can the spiritual dimension of life contribute to the needs that marriage addresses?

4. How can we train our young adult children to be more discerning in finding a life partner?
5. What are some practical ways we can help our twenty-something children after they are married?

STRENGTHEN
1. As you perceive things, what is your child's greatest need related to personal relationships? What should you do to help?

{10} SOUL PROVIDERS

START
1. What are some of the challenges that churches face in reaching twenty-somethings?

STUDY
1. What factors seem to be attracting young adults to traditional Christian faith?
2. As a whole, is this generation a churchgoing one? What factors are having the greatest influence?
3. How can we model a positive faith for our children to follow?
4. What are the elements of a strong personal testimony? What is your testimony?
5. Toward which elements of a nontraditional church should we draw our children's attention? Why?
6. What are the hopeful signs for spiritual strength among this young generation?

STRENGTHEN

1. How would you describe the spiritual maturity of your child? What do you think is your best approach for helping him or her grow in this area?

{11} WAITING FOR THE FUTURE

START

1. How do you imagine your child's life twenty years from now?

STUDY

1. Why are our children our most significant legacy?
2. What is involved in shaping the legacy of character?
3. How can you use love as a foundational legacy for your child?
4. The sculptor Michelangelo could see an "angel" within his block of stone. How can you maintain your faith in the potential of your child?
5. What is the most powerful force in the world?

STRENGTHEN

1. What is the single most important message you personally received from this book? How will you apply it to parenting your young adult child?

CHAPTER 1

1. Elina Furman, *Boomerang Nation: How to Survive Living with Your Parents . . . The Second Time Around* (New York: Simon and Schuster, 2005).
2. Alexandra Robbins and Abby Wilner, *Quarterlife Crisis: The Unique Challenges of Life in Your Twenties* (New York: Tarcher/Putnam, 2001).
3. Cited in Furman, *Boomerang Nation*.
4. Ibid., 10.
5. Research by the Barna Research Group, at http://www.barna.org/FlexPage.aspx?Page=BarnaUpdate&BarnaUpdateID=149.

CHAPTER 4

1. From Dr. Arnett's Web site at http://jeffreyarnett.com/articles.htm.
2. See http://www.usatoday.com/life/lifestyle/2004-09-30-extended-adolescence_x.htm.

CHAPTER 5

1. Press release from the Centers for Disease Control and Prevention, at http:www/cdc.gov/od/oc/media/pressrel/r041202.htm.
2. C. Ogden, M. Carroll, et al., "Prevalence of Overweight and Obesity in the United States, 1999–2004," *Journal of the American Medical Association*, 2006; 295:1549–55.

3. Sleep in America, 2003 National Sleep Foundation Poll," News Release, National Sleep Foundation, at http://www.sleep foundation.org/hottopics/index.php?secid=16&id=371.

CHAPTER 6

1. Keturah Gray, "Quarterlife Crisis Hits Many in Late 20s," ABC News Career Center, at http://abcnews.go.com/Business/Careers/story?id=688240&page=1.
2. Ibid.
3. Alexandra Robbins and Abby Wilner, *Quarterlife Crisis: The Unique Challenges of Life in Your Twenties* (New York: Tarcher/Putnam, 2001), 165.
4. Colin Allen, "When Worry Takes Over," *Psychology Today*, June 10, 2003, at www.psychologytoday.com.
5. Marilyn Elias, "Childhood Depression," *USA Today*, August 13, 1998, 2D.
6. Catherine Siskos, "Don't Get Sick—Twentysomethings Uninsured," *Kiplinger's Personal Finance*, July 2000, at http://www.badfaithinsurance.org/reference/HL/0087a.htm.
7. Ibid.

CHAPTER 7

1. Story cited in Dr. Larry V. Stockman and Cynthia S. Graves, *Grown-Up Children Who Won't Grow Up: How to Finally Cut the Cord That Binds You* (Rocklin, CA: Prima, 1994), 105–6.
2. Peg Tyre, "Bringing Up Adultolescents," *Newsweek*, March 25, 2002, at http://www.newsweek.com.
3. These figures, which are subject to change, are taken from Elina Furman, *Boomerang Nation*, 158–59.

CHAPTER 8

1. Jenny Hedden, *Twentysomethings: Managing the New Breed of Employee*, from the newsletter *Restaurants USA*, September 1996, cited at http://www.restaurant.org.
2. Ibid.

3. Ibid.
4. Peter W. Stevenson, "Peace Corps Applications Soar," at www.cbsnews.com, July 28, 2006.
5. Beth Walton, "Volunteer Rates Hit Record Number," *USA Today*, July 7, 2006.
6. "Burnout: To Change Careers or Not Change Careers? That Is the Question," uncredited Associated Press story, December 31, 2005.
7. Lev Grossman, "Grow Up? Not So Fast," *Time*, January 24, 2005, 54.
8. Ibid., 47.

CHAPTER 9

1. Barbara Dafoe Whitehead and David Popenoe, "Who Wants to Marry a Soul Mate?: New Survey Findings on Young Adults' Attitudes About Love and Marriage," copyright © 2001 by the National Marriage Project, at http://marriage.rutgers.edu/.
2. Shel Silverstein, *The Missing Piece* (New York: HarperCollins, 1976).
3. Grossman, "Grow Up?," 49.

CHAPTER 10

1. Agnieszka Tennant, "The Good News About Generations X & Y," *Christianity Today*, August 5, 2002; at http://www.christianitytoday.com/ct/2002/009/3.40.html.
2. Ibid.
3. "Twentysomethings Struggle to Find Their Place in Christian Churches," The Barna Update, found at http://www.barna.org/FlexPage.aspx?Page=BarnaUpdate&BarnaUpdateID=149.
4. Ibid.

{about the author}

ROSS CAMPBELL, M.D. has spent more than 30 years as a clinical psychiatrist, concentrating on the parent-child relationship. Formerly an associate clinical professor of pediatrics and psychiatry at the University of Tennessee College of Medicine, Dr. Campbell has counseled thousands of parents throughout his extensive career. Today he writes and lectures on parenting topics.